NORTHERN ORCHARDS

Places Near the Dead

NORTHERN ORCHARDS
Places Near the Dead

James Silas Rogers

North Star Press of St. Cloud
2014

ISBN 978-0-87839-762-4

First Edition: May 2014

Printed in the United States of America

Published by
North Star Press of St. Cloud, Inc.
P.O. Box 451
St. Cloud, Minnesota 56302

www.northstarpress.com

Front cover design by Jennifer Osborne Anderson
Book design and book production by Judy Gilats

for Michael Coady

Sláinte na mbeo is na marbh:

To the health of the living and the dead.

CONTENTS

AMONG NORTHERN ORCHARDS

According to the historian Kenneth Jackson in *Silent Cities: A History of the American Cemetery*, there are a minimum of 500,000 marked burial grounds in the United States. America thus holds two-and-a-half times as many cemeteries as it does gas stations, more than three times as many cemeteries as convenience stores, and about fourteen times as many cemeteries as movie screens.

If we look closely, we all occupy places near the dead. This collection is about my experiences of a few of the half-million or so places that announce themselves as burial grounds.

Cemeteries are almost always unsurprising places. I like them that way. Quite a few books have been published that have gathered together humorous epitaphs, and at one time or another we have all seen such memorial oddments as the marble statue of the man with his golf clubs in Indiana, and the granite Mercedes-Benz over the grave of a young man in New Jersey. These things bore me.

Nor am I especially interested in the biographical and genealogical dimensions of cemeteries. When I would tell people I was writing a book about cemeteries, they would inevitably want to tell me about a man or woman of historic significance buried in this place or that. (Once, in Wayne, Michigan, a groundskeeper preemptively stopped our car to let us know where the grave of Jackie Wilson, "Mr. Entertainment," was to be found.) It's a rare burial ground that does not contain someone linked to a famous or ought-to-be-famous individual. Such ties are diverting, but usually seem to me to trivialize the great sweep of both great and the obscure presences that make up any burial ground. I think my favorite old graveyard is Hope Cemetery in Galesburg, Illinois, which is just down the street from where my daughter went to college. I was delighted to discover that the man who invented the first metal Ferris Wheel is buried there, and also that it is the burial ground of the poet Julia Fletcher

Carney who lived across the street from the young Carl Sandburg and whose widely anthologized poem from 1845, "Little Things" ("Little drops of water / Little grains of sand / Make the mighty ocean / And the happy land") is one that my grandmother used to recite. But those associations are not why I love Hope Cemetery. I love it because of its gentle hillsides, because of the way its headstones tilt gently this way or that but still stand strong; I love it, too, because of the scuff of curling elm leaves underfoot in November.

I do think there are places that can lead us beyond ourselves, where a sensation of connectedness and transcendence comes readily. I find nothing macabre in visiting, hanging around in, or writing about cemeteries; on the contrary, I find it ennobling.

The novelist Elizabeth Bowen wrote that cemeteries are places of "restored innocence" and, though I'm not completely sure I know what she meant, it sounds right. The phrase I keep coming back to, when I reflect on cemeteries, is "the sacramentality of place." For one thing, graveyards and church sanctuaries are pretty much the last places left in contemporary America that successfully resist advertising and commercialization: that alone counts as a spiritual experience. But the transcendent character of burial places rest on something deeper, I think. Bowen's observation about restored innocence puts me in mind of the Catholic sacraments with which I have grown up: baptism that links dying with new life, confession that binds together recall and forgiveness. Cemeteries do that for us, too. They are places we go to remember, but also places where we discover—in words of the Irish poet Michael Coady to whom this book is dedicated—that "it is in remembering that / little by little / we are allowed to forget."

Abstraction isn't helpful to memory. Remembrance attaches itself to specifics. That house, that back door; this elm tree, this hillside, this headstone.

In the short term, before the long erosion of forgetting begins its natural processes, our individual memories inscribe places with memory. My elderly mother announced, at age ninety, that she'd like to be cremated, a wish we will have to implement sooner instead of later; she is ninety-seven at the time of this writing. There are lots of good arguments in favor of the practice—my mother, being pragmatic and unsentimental, makes the economic case—and her ashes will be interred alongside my late father. I would prefer a traditional burial; but we will honor her wishes, and I am glad my mother's remains will not be scattered to the wind. At Oak Hill Cemetery in the city of South St. Paul where she lived most of her life, there will be a place that is always hers, a place that for those of us left behind will always be different from any other in the world. Place is one of the things that makes us human, that makes us larger than ourselves; as Scott Russell Sanders wrote in *Staying Put*, "We marry ourselves to the cosmos by knowing and cherishing a particular place, just as we join ourselves to the human family by marrying a particular man or woman." Or, he might have added, by being buried there.

Finally, a few words on nomenclature. Though I have used the three terms "cemetery," "graveyard," and "burial ground" interchangeably, properly speaking the last term is the most accurate. To be called a graveyard, the site should adjoin a church. "Cemetery" was a nineteenth-century neologism that stems from the Greek word for a sleeping chamber, and as such it carries a weight of avoidance and euphemism. "Burial ground" is thus the most accurate term. To be honest, the term I like best is a colloquialism that I've only heard used by my late father's best friend (a hard-drinking railroad man named O'Gara), who always spoke of cemeteries as "marble orchards." I thought that was great bit of folk poetry when I first heard it fifty years ago, and his laconic phrase is still rattling around behind the title of this collection.

— ST. PAUL, MINNESOTA

THE YOUNG BIRDWATCHER

When May got most ripe
we visited Acacia Park.
Grandma hauled a tub
of lilacs on her hip

cut to dress Preston's
and Granny Wigginton's graves
and that of Evans Rogers,
dead since 1936.

Adults looked after flowers
while we roamed about,
understanding not to run
down cemetery hills, or shout.

Women who knew the dead
kept their calendar;
I kept my own.
Each year this visit meant

I'd spot gold- and ruby-
crowned kinglets—
almost the smallest of birds,
hardly bigger than moths—

stopped on their flight
north, in the windbreak
row of spruces
near my uncle's grave.

They would flit in and out
while the women brushed away
matted grass, fussed,
and then stood silent,

as I imagined deep Canada
where kinglets nest:
an endless pine-blue forest
filled with such birds,

the cold upper reach
of a continent
in which even the treetops
know only shade.

ELEGY

Highland Cemetery occupies a knoll at the intersection of County Roads 31 and 42, three miles southwest of the town of Rosemount, Minnesota, about seventeen miles from the Twin Cities. A new road, open for traffic soon, has been graded near the cemetery's boundary.

A fence of long iron pipes held in place by posts the size of railroad ties delineates the northern edge of the cemetery. The pipes, unpainted for many years, wear a lustrous coat of rust. Poke your finger at points where they have rusted through, though, and the metal will flake away like dry clay. Deep fissures run down the sides of the wooden posts. Sections of the fence pull away from one another and tilt toward the ground. The fence serves only to show the man who occasionally tends the cemetery where to stop mowing.

Church archives record 260 burials in Highland Cemetery—including that of F. Scott Fitzgerald's immigrant great-grandmother McQuillan— though other graves almost certainly went unmarked in its earliest days. The last person interred here was a woman named Kate Fahey, born in County Mayo, Ireland, in 1883. A widow, she ran a boardinghouse in a nearby town and died in 1947. Most graves in Highland Cemetery date from the first eleven years after it opened in 1868, and nearly all of those buried here were Irish, often from the Western counties of Mayo and Galway. William B. O'Donoghue, buried here, was a Fenian rebel who, in 1867, brought his campaign against Britain to Minnesota by invading Canada with an army of thirty-five men. After being pursued by American forces who had crossed the border, O'Donoghue fled south to Rosemount—an Irish farming community at the time—where he taught school. The townspeople took up a collection to buy a monument after his early death. His headstone reads defiantly: "He loved liberty and hated oppression, therefore he died in exile."

Rural Americans of the nineteenth century often ordered gravestones from Sears, Roebuck and other mail-order firms, and sometimes a typographical error would arrive enshrined in marble; here, the hero's name is misspelled as "O'Donohue." On the Sheridan family headstone a few yards away, the letter N has been carved backward, as if the stonecutter were dyslectic.

The cemetery's name reflects not only the modest elevation of its site, but also the Highland or Hyland family name (both variants appear on headstones). In the past, family members believed that an ancestor had donated the cemetery land to St. Joseph's Catholic church, the parish responsible for the graveyard. Father Thomas Hill, the current pastor, denies this and points to a bill of sale still held by the parish. Father Hill often finds himself negotiating between conflicting ideas about the past, present, and future of the cemetery. The parish's maintenance person once told a member of the Hyland family that he hoped in thirty years the cemetery would be completely flat, easy to mow, with maybe a plaque to note where the graves used to be.

The Hyland family retains undisputed ties of ancestry to the cemetery and in 1999 restored the granite monument on their family plot. Few other monuments in the cemetery have received any recent attention, however, except—according to the charges of concerned descendants— for those knocked over or damaged by a front-end loader hired by the parish to "remodel" the cemetery in 1998. Hill points out that the unstable headstones in the graveyard presented a potential liability and insists there were numerous committee meetings and other forums within the parish during which the families could have contributed to a discussion about the site's future. The families say they were never consulted. The parish's legal and traditional obligations to the cemetery exceed any emotional connection. Of the fourteen hundred families currently registered at St. Joseph's parish, no more than a half dozen have relatives buried in Highland Cemetery.

Shawne FitzGerald of Minneapolis, a Hyland descendant, has a website devoted to the graveyard. It includes all of the inscriptions on the headstones, a cemetery map, photographs, and links to short histories of the various families taken from the research of a dogged genealogist, Kevin Geraghty of St. Paul, whose great-grandparents are buried there. The website presents an indignant account of the parish-sponsored remodeling of the cemetery. In September 1998, the parish regraded the cemetery and the traditional cast-iron palings and chain fences around several early plots were uprooted and demolished. Pieces of many fractured headstones disappeared. FitzGerald thinks they may be buried under piles of brush and clippings at the back of the lot. A new entrance road was graded to allow access for large machinery, which, she charges, runs over the unmarked grave of a child.

The website exhorts the public to contact the archbishop, the archdiocesan Catholic Cemeteries office, and the pastor to protest the condition of Highland Cemetery. When pressed about the controversies that have lately surrounded the site, Father Hill asks—in a clearly bemused tone—where were the families during the years that the archdiocese listed the cemetery as abandoned?

Since 1980, I have published a number of pieces on the history of the Irish in Minnesota, including a calendar that printed the only known photograph of the rebel O'Donoghue. I had been to Highland Cemetery twenty years ago, doing research for that project, but my recent interest in the site came about through my friend Dermot O'Mara. Like many Irish people, Dermot has the quality of being simultaneously pragmatic and idealistic. When he chanced on this old Irish graveyard in late March 2000, he grew concerned about its imperiled condition, and—though he has no familial reason for sentiment—started calling people to see if something might be done to protect and restore it. When Dermot called me, I remembered little except the site's isolation and openness to the wind. It had been a February afternoon when I visited the cemetery two decades earlier, and the wind came sweeping in from the western prairies, a wind that had passed over no towns of more than a few thousand souls.

Dermot moved to Minnesota from Cork, Ireland, in 1984. He has prospered in the United States, where he runs an Irish gift shop from a freestanding home on Grand Avenue, St. Paul's most desirable retail district. The shop includes an art gallery and boasts of offering the largest selection of traditional music in North America. With his American wife, Molly Lynch, last summer Dermot became a parent at the age of thirty-seven. When I met him at his home before going to the cemetery, his ten-month-old daughter, Emer, was getting a bath in the sink. Recently he began making arrangements to sell his business in order to resettle on a farm in County Galway.

Two days after Memorial Day, on an evening with low clouds and rain spitting—cool, Irish weather, though this was May in Minnesota—Dermot and I drove to Highland Cemetery. Northern Dakota County comprises one of the most youthful and fast-growing parts of the metropolitan area, but apart from an occasional rollerblader striding and swaying in time to the music on a Walkman, we saw almost no one on the newly paved trails that parallel County 31. Tracts of new homes and townhouse developments with such names at Kingswood Ponds, Wood-Winds, and Emerald Pond Estates cluster along the road, with convenience stores, strip malls, and pay-at-the-pump gas stations.

As we drove, Dermot asked about various places and points of local history. A strong sense of both history and of community shine through in Dermot. At times, he gives the impression he feels himself to be not only a citizen of Ireland or of America, but also a citizen of history itself. Dermot's plan to return to Ireland stems in part from his wish to give his daughter a sense of historical continuity.

When Dermot first saw Highland Cemetery, he was distressed by the neglect of the site and even more distressed to learn that a strip mall would soon be built fifty yards north of the Irish pioneer graves. In two or three years, young people will cut through the graveyard on their way to rent videos; they will toss plastic soda bottles and empty Whopper boxes among the headstones. Dermot hopes to encourage the Irish people in Minnesota to take up the graveyard's precarious condition as a *cause célèbre*.

I have long known the area through which we drove, as I grew up in what is now Inver Grove Heights (the next community north of Rosemount) on the very frontier of the suburbs, in a 1957 split-level rambler, which, at the time it was built, stood across the road from a cornfield. As a teenager, I bicycled practically every road in northern Dakota County. If I did not bicycle on them, I rode on them with my father on summer evenings; he liked to stop at roadside ponds and watch waterfowl and egrets. On a thousand such drives, my father would remark, *I remember when this land was just farm country*. This evening I found myself extending the same theme. As we approached the cemetery, I remembered a German shepherd loose in a farmyard, and how I had pedaled to outrun it. A Conoco station now stands near that farm.

The rain let up as Dermot and I arrived. He parked his car far on the shoulder across County Road 31. I noted a surveyor's stake, with an orange plastic ribbon tied to it, pounded in the roadside right-of-way. We let traffic pass, then ran across the road and up a gentle slope to the gravesites. Lawn grass is not the natural vegetation here, as the site has no water; grass competes with—and loses to—stringy, tough-stemmed weeds. The usual roadside detritus of fading soft-drink cups and plastic straws blows up the slope and snags in the milkweed and Queen Anne's Lace. There was farmland directly across the road, and beyond it stood hundreds of new homes, each painted slate blue or earthy brown. The earth itself—at least the field newly planted just to the south and in the field across the street—looked worn, the soil bleached. Nonetheless, rows of corn sprouted.

"Those are probably the last crops that will ever be planted here," Dermot said. He pointed to the future building site, a plowed field of perhaps seventy acres. Beyond the field, a duck slough hid behind a copse of trees. As a boy in the 1960s and 1970s, I watched nascent suburban creep claim one after another of these wetlands. Progress: If this were thirty years ago the lake would have been drained to make way for houses. Today's developers are mandated by law to protect the lake, and they probably also see it as a bit of rural charm. One can imagine the coined street names that will go into the new development: Cattail Path, Teal Way, Duck Pass Court. Developers would never incorporate the features of this small knoll into their lexicon of place, though, because the places they build consciously ignore the past. "A suburb," writes the poet Eavan Boland, "is all about futures. Trees grow; a small car becomes a bigger one to accommodate new arrivals . . . there is little enough history, almost no appeal to memory." Headstone Way? Cemetery Trail? Not likely.

Dermot and I stood looking at the landscape, and I thought that if my father, born in 1913, were alive, he could tell you where he used to shoot prairie chickens within sight of this hillside. Though attenuated, I also sense a historical connection to this area through the stories he told me of his bygone hunting trips, how Elmer so-and-so used to let him hunt on this farm, how his brother once stood on that road and shot three pheasants before closing the car door. Another history may also be unfolding here, a history I cannot claim as my own because I am too close to it, a history shared by millions of Americans: We have witnessed America transform itself into a suburban culture.

"At the very least," Dermot said, "there needs to be a good strong fence around this cemetery so that no one comes in here with a four-wheel-drive truck to tear though the headstones."

Nothing stands between the road and the graves. Something felt wrong. Simply by being left vulnerable to the world outside, this site—where we had every reason to expect a sense of enclosure and protectedness, a sense of sacred space—had already been vandalized.

Chunks of limestone or marble leaned in a clutter at the base of many of the markers. There were shards of crosses and broken urns that would have crowned the headstones when new. Many older stones had been laid flat and made flush with the ground, and we speculated that this was a recent measure; the carvings and inscriptions were too well preserved to have lain under many Minnesota winters. Mats of grass clippings spread over the edges of these embedded headstones, filling them in like putty around a window glazing.

Dermot examined the weathering on a white obelisk bearing the name McGrath. Using the flat edge of a car key, he scraped off a coin-sized mound of lichen and held it tentatively in the palm of his hand, as if it might be toxic. He had not seen lichen like this before. Lichen spores cling to porous stones like those used for monuments a century ago. Lichen grows slowly, but once established it's hard to remove. Decade by decade, green-gold splotches accrue on the white marble.

The early settlers usually aligned the headstones to face east. In the lee of 130 years of winter storms most of them remained legible, though it took us a long time to discern the name on the base of a small gray marker before deciding it read McCarthy. The McCarthy stone cannot be read at all if looked at it straight on, but from the top down, the carvings inscribed when Grover Cleveland was president leave interpretable shadows. "Probably a Cork man," Dermot said.

I wondered how long it takes for a name to be severed from a place, for McCarthy to no longer be a Cork name, or a Rosemount farmer's name, or even the name of someone's grandfather, a grandfather who had a face and pocketknife and a house with a cottonwood tree in the yard.

As long as it takes for a headstone to become unreadable?

As long as it has taken family farming to dwindle away?

As long as it takes to buy lunch at Burger King?

Dermot and I continued to walk, weaving in and out of the lanes, reading names, dates, and inscriptions half to ourselves and half aloud: Quigley, McQuillan, Casey, Bambery, Lenehan, Lynch. Mayo, Limerick, Galway, Mayo again. It struck me that probably no one in this cemetery ever returned to Ireland after leaving it.

"Look at this fellow, here," Dermot said, stopping before an impressive granite stone, one of the few in the cemetery to have retained its finial cross. "James Dewire, born County Galway 1832, died 10 July 1872. Do you think he's the same family as the Dwyers buried over there? He would have been an Irish-speaker who lived through the Famine."

Dermot looked at the heavy equipment parked on the new road to the north and said quietly, "Whoever he was, he didn't grub out the trees and clear the field of rocks for this."

For this. I began pulling weeds from around an 1886 grave and thought about what Dermot meant by "this." The headstones had been laid flat, and the floral carvings had begun to cup soil, giving a clump of weeds a place to take root on the stone itself.

I absentmindedly broke off a piece of wild yarrow and started to chew it, then spit out the bitter weed. If "this" meant new homes in a safe neighborhood, then Dermot was, at one level, completely wrong. The affluence that makes possible these suburbs is precisely what the people buried here wanted for their children and grandchildren, a nineteenth-century midwest variation on Thomas Jefferson's pronouncement that he was a farmer so that his son could be a gentleman.

Except, except, except: I knew Dermot was right. James Dewire didn't grub out trees to make a farm so that, 128 years after his death, it could be paved over to build Taco Bells and Arbys and surrendered to put up new homes with SUVs in the driveway and bass boats in the garage. Behind the disdain in Dermot's phrase "for this" lay an intuition that the life being bought with these new homes is just too easy. This, too, is a presence that filled this graveyard: the dignity of rest well earned. When we lose agricultural land, part of what gets ruptured and sent into the wind is the spirit of the work that went into the vanished farm.

The occasional rain turned to drizzle, and we headed for Dermot's car. "It would be a shame, he said, "if we let this place be forgotten."

I began to suggest possible projects. Maybe we could lobby, or raise money, to get a fence put up. Maybe we could get the historical society to erect a roadside marker about the rural Irish. Maybe we could organize an Irish poetry reading among the headstones, a walking tour for school children. Even as I warmed to these ideas, part of me knew they would amount to little. The future of this cemetery will be, by definition, anomalous and ornamental.

As we walked toward the car, I thought of how strange it would seem to many that we would even care about this place. Dermot was born in Ireland. He has no people in this cemetery. I was born and raised fewer than ten miles from here. I have no people in this cemetery.

Except for everyone.

From the roadside litter I picked up a fading soft drink cup from the PDQ convenience store up the road.

Pretty. Damned. Quick.

A red Jeep sped past us on the soon-to-be-enlarged highway, its stereo so loud that the surge of its notes preceded it like a siren.

AT A COUNTRY GRAVEYARD
IN WASHINGTON COUNTY

A nesting chipping sparrow
enters a juniper.
Small insects hop
underfoot in the drying sod.

The German farmers here
died in their own language.
On headstones,
only the years make sense.

Along the road,
a trail of snapped-off butterflies;
like unmoored sailboats,
their fading, ragged wings

draw tight
and tilt in the breeze,
shards of a summer prayer
that never got heard.

TO THE SCULPTOR WHO CARVED
THE HEADSTONE OF JAMES CHARLIS,
BORN IN KELLS, COUNTY MEATH, IN 1796

When sacred artists write an icon
they believe it incomplete, until
Greek letters fix it before God;

though I distrust words as I walk
among chiseled, fading names
on this fog-damped hill,

where the part that lives still
at James Charlis's grave
is a barrel-chested Christ: sandstone,

not Italian marble, and carved
with whatever tools were at hand.
His dwarf-heavy head falls

well short of the cross-bar
toward which his blunt arms stretch,
pinned in place by dull

nails—a misshapen figure
entirely of this world,
that somehow mirrors a soul.

Bless your hand, who worked
this stubby Christ. Whoever you were,
you lacked the artist's usual skills

of deception. And bless
the wounded grace of this figure,
its holy clumsiness,

just as we bless and thank
the gaunt monks whose quills
drew the wide-eyed savior

in that book a Welshman
thought angelic.
The man below was also a child of Kells.

ROADS, STORIES, INDIANS, AIR

We go to cemeteries, in part, to realign ourselves with the stories we have already received. This is especially true if we have bonds of ancestry and recollection with someone buried there; but even when we lack such connections, we can go to cemeteries in order to wait for other peoples' stories. Most gravestones provide at the very least a protagonist, a beginning, and an end, and one of the odd things about cemeteries is that even this minimalist narrative seems strangely complete. Somehow, the mere act of encountering name after name on headstones, even when they are unknown to us—or maybe it's precisely because we must confront the reality that the named individuals can never become familiar—allow these places of memory and forgetfulness to make a claim on us. In that way, I suppose, cemeteries become in the end places where we go to wait for our own story.

I think about stories whenever I pass Pilot Knob, a prominence of land (the highest in southern Minnesota) at the south end of the Mendota Bridge, ten miles from the Minneapolis city center. Five of my forebears—my paternal grandparents, one set of great-grandparents, and an uncle who died in the Far East during Word War II—are buried in Acacia Park, a cemetery that has crowned the hill since 1928. I only knew one of those relatives, my Grandmother Rogers, and she didn't die until I was twenty years old: but long before her death, I knew Pilot Knob as a place where traffic halted.

When I was a boy, my family often made weekend visits to my maternal grandparents in Green Isle, a small town about seventy miles southwest of the Twin Cities. My maternal grandmother would often decide to come back with us. She was a haughty and a slow-moving woman who would not be hurried. It always took her a long time to get moving, and so on the way home we would usually get caught in Sunday evening traffic on Minnesota Highway 13. My father would find himself stuck behind a cattle truck headed to South St. Paul for the opening of the livestock markets Monday morning. He couldn't pass and couldn't see around the trucks, and he would cuss and swear about the "goddamned bull haulers" on the road.

About seven miles from home, we would wait in the snarl of traffic where Highway 13 crossed Highway 55. Both roads have since been redesigned as freeways that glide over one another, but in those days cars would back up and take what seemed like hours to get through the intersection. The headlights on the bridge poured past like flood waters down an aqueduct. We kids, either half asleep or restless, or sometimes carsick, would watch as my dad lit cigarettes off the glowing coils of the dashboard lighter, and he would fume as the standstill continued. Inevitably on these Sunday nights my small-town grandmother would look at the streams of white and red lights going by and say in amazement, "And they all know their names, and they all know where they're going."

Decades later, her statement still carries a specific meaning in my family: my grandmother's remark *They all know where they're going* has come to be a shorthand for a self-evident, sentencious observation. That seems a bit unfair to my grandmother: I thought then, and I still think, that it *is* remarkable that hundreds, thousands, tens of thousands of drivers, each with a separate origin, purpose, and destination, can engage in the shared experience of driving on a busy road and yet remain discreet and unconnected to all the others. It is one of those marvels of complexity that make a world.

Lately I have been driving over the Mendota Bridge with some frequency, on my way out to visit the cemetery or the Pilot Knob region, in which I've taken a preservationist's interest, and I smile when I recall my grandmother's remark. *They all know where they're going.* Then I turn right at the Acacia Boulevard exit, and drive to the cemetery. For some reason, it feels more ceremonious and proper to park a few blocks from the gates and enter Acacia Park on foot.

Like the more famous Forest Lawn in California (with which it is a near contemporary), Acacia Park is an early "memorial park." In such burial grounds, the landscape itself serves as the artistic tribute to the dead; the management allows only markers that lie flush with the ground.

It makes for a graceful lawn, but it also permits untended markers to be obscured by thick mats of grass clippings. When I check on my family gravesites, I often kneel and tear away the accrued clippings. Without such attention, a layer of new sod would form over the bronze plaques within a few years, as it has on gravesite after gravesite on Pilot Knob.

Last March, I had a hard time finding the family plot, and I told myself that next time I would bring along a pocketknife and properly trim away the new growth. But on this cold spring afternoon, I pulled it out with my hands. As I ripped away thatch from the plaque that marks the burial site of my great-grandfather, Spencer Obed Wigginton, I thought of how little I really knew of him: he was a small-town pharmacist, and after he lost everything in a fire back in Kentucky, he had to move north to live with his daughter. He knew Chandler, the man who invented Coca-Cola.

Only the letters "IGGIN" could be seen on the grave of my great-grandmother, Elizabeth Calvert Wigginton, and what I know of her was that she was an impetuous, meddlesome person. She once peeked in a neighbor's refrigerator and a roast fell out on the floor and was ruined; and when my grandmother was a teenaged girl, Granny Wigginton snatched a novel out of her hands and burned it because she had heard it mentioned a divorced woman. I tore the thatch away to reveal her full name.

Here was my grandfather, Evans Rogers, who died sixteen years before I was born. My father often hinted that he had been very strict, but what I know for certain is that my grandfather sold hogs in the South St. Paul stockyards, and that he once lost money by investing in miniature golf.

Then my uncle Preston, an Army Air Force master sergeant who contracted jungle rot after serving in combat in the Philippines, died on a troop ship on the way home. His death was the great sadness of my grandmother's life. On a May evening in 1945 she received a telegram that she thought was from Preston, reporting that he had landed safely in California but which instead came from the secretary of war. I cleaned away the perimeter of his grave marker.

My hands were dirty and cold. I did the same for my grandmother, Mary Edna Wigginton, from whom all of these stories and fragments of stories have come down. For twenty years, I'd sat on my grandmother's couch and listened to her, and soon I began to fill in more details about the simple names on the bronzes in front of me: my grandfather's love of harness racing; the fact that my uncle's nickname was "Pill"; my great-grandmother's famous biscuits from scratch. I feel fortunate to be heir to the stories that have endured.

The morning hours are lovely in Acacia Park, when the air is apt to be filled with birdsong. On spring mornings, there are usually several people in the cemetery at 7:30 or so, and most of them have binoculars around their necks. Migrating birds still follow their ancient flyways; bird-watchers can almost count on spotting an interesting species there. One morning when I was walking there I told a cluster of birders that I had seen a loggerhead shrike a few days earlier, and they all set off like a posse to a nearby line of spruce trees.

But the sunset hour is when Pilot Knob is at its best. If the trees are not in leaf, you can walk to the northern edge of the cemetery and look over the expanse of the Mendota Bridge. The bridge stretches four-fifths of a mile across the Minnesota River valley, north-to-south, and the evening sun casts a gold luster on its thirteen arches. When it opened in 1926, and for some time after that, the Mendota Bridge was the largest poured-concrete structure in the world. It remains impressive and, as with many grand structures, there is an unseen portion that is in its own way even more dazzling; in this case, footings that extend 320 feet through alluvial silt before they finally come to rest on bedrock.

Most people who are in Acacia Park at sunset will look to the west, though. At the very top of the hill there is a small stone bench that seems to have been placed with the sunset view in mind. In front of this bench lies the daredevil aviator Speed Holman, who was for a long time the most celebrated person interred at Acacia Park. (That distinction now surely goes to nine-time presidential candidate Harold Stassen, who lies only a few yards away from the aviator.) Holman died young, in a crash at the Omaha Air Show in 1932. The downtown airport in St Paul is named for him; outside its terminal there is a monument that declares, "He Belonged to the Heights and the Heights Claimed Him" which is a poetic, if slightly nonsensical thought—for what claimed him was, precisely, the ground. According to one story, the first time Holman flew over Pilot Knob, when he came down he told friends it was so beautiful it was where he'd like to be buried.

From Holman's grave, you have a perfect view of the sun as it sinks further and further toward the horizon, and darkness starts to fill in the Minnesota River bottoms. Some trick of light or perspective works on that western slope; in June it seems as if a rich, buttery gold is welling up from the low-lying areas, and at the same time as if the land itself is sinking, surrendering to darkness. Finally the sun drops behind the international airport located a mile to the northwest. This is one of the moments when the loveliness in and around Acacia Park still lives up to a 1935 promotional brochure that declared, "If you would be impressed, journey some twilight hour to Pilot Knob. It is a place for those who write verse on the beauty Nature has given us. There—high above the Minnesota and Mississippi rivers is unfolded a wealth of charming views, quiet, restful, and beautiful."

Most of the time, though, restfulness seems far away. The Indian name for Pilot Knob—*O-be-ya-wa-be,* or "hill that is much visited"—is not especially accurate; it definitely could be called a hill that is much bypassed. The Minneapolis-St Paul Airport just across the river is the eleventh busiest airport in the world. Planes pass overhead—one after another, at some times of day—at altitudes of 500 to 600 feet. Burial services at Acacia Park Cemetery often need to halt until overflight noise subsides. And Pilot Knob is surrounded by a commuter landscape; roads of all sizes criss-cross the adjoining lands. Minnesota Department of Transportation statistics count an average of 40,000 cars a day on Highway 55, and another 7,000 on Highway 13, which it intersects. An 1887 map give the French name for *O-be-ya-wa-be* as "La buttes des Morte," or "hill of the dead"; for all the repose within the cemetery, the fact is that the edges of this landform of stillness now teem like an anthill.

Perhaps I am drawn to places like Pilot Knob—places that manage to resist the clamor of civilization—because of my father. There was something in him that resonated with Daniel Boone's supposed axiom that when he could smell the smoke from his neighbors' chimney, it was time to move. Of course, my father never actually moved; his yearning for solitude pretty much took the form of a lifelong complaint that there were just too damned many people. When he died in 1974, the book on his bedside was a travelogue about vanishing places titled *What's Left.* I started going out to Pilot Knob regularly when I learned that it, too, might be overrun by the anthill, a prospect that came back into my awareness forcefully when one December morning, I opened the Minneapolis paper and read a letter to the editor protesting a housing development proposed for the properties that adjoin Acacia Park.

The letter's author, Jeremy Hubbell, a Ph.D. student in urban history whose dissertation project is a history of early Minneapolis, is especially interested in Highway 55, the road that passes Pilot Knob. I found Jeremy's name in the phone book, and we met for coffee not long after that, where he briefed me on the background to the story. A real estate developer, Ron Clark Construction and Design, wishes to construct a string of town homes immediately east of the cemetery and a smaller number of expensive luxury homes immediately atop the bluff, which would effectively privatize the view. A coalition of preservationists, Native Americans, and concerned citizens who object to these plans has been lobbying the Mendota Heights city council to reject the proposal. I attended a council meeting on a cold January night, and was surprised to find that more than two hundred persons had turned out to testify in favor of an environmental impact study. The most substantive testimony at that meeting came from Bruce White, an independent historian who specializes in Native American matters. He had prepared a comprehensive, thirty-two-page summary that clearly demonstrated that "Pilot Knob— including the entire ridge or bluff—is a historically important area." The question hardly needs debating. The City of Mendota Heights's own website already proclaims that the hill "is unusual in the broad scope of its historic significance," and in 1931 the Daughters of the American Revolution mounted a plaque on the summit to commemorate the signing of a treaty with the Mdewakanton Sioux on this site in 1851. Like every treaty between whites and Indians, the agreement was about more than just the sale of land; it was about the implied surrender of all that inhered in the land.

The city council voted to require the study. Their questions of Dr. White (he holds a doctorate in historical anthropology) focused chiefly on whether or not the region was known to contain Indian bones, which it does. For now, the developer's plans to build on the open space adjoining Acacia Park Cemetery have been stalled, if not permanently halted. I've read much of the literature on which the report was based, and remain optimistic about the future of the site. If bones are what it takes to prove historicity, there is plenty of written evidence. The memoirs of the

Bernier family, who were longtime French Canadian shopkeepers in Mendota tell of digging up arrowheads and Indian remains in their garden. For that matter, when the Masonic Order developed the Acacia property in 1928, at least some Indian remains were discovered, and, according to a contemporary account, "laid to rest elsewhere until some future time when with befitting ceremonies they will be re-interred near their old resting places."

And yet, the line of thought that pins the specialness of Pilot Knob on the presence of bone misses a larger point: that it is far more likely *O-be-ya-wa-be* presented a sacred character before anyone—white or native— was ever buried there. City councils, planning boards, and especially, real estate developers have a hard time making room for even the existence of sacred places, though such places persist over centuries, and by no means do all of them contain bones. White people opened this cemetery in 1926, but for centuries before the arrival of settlers, and indeed for half a century after the frontier soldier Lt. Zebulon Pike first mapped it, the Mdewakanton Sioux used this hilltop as a place to raise the bodies of their dead as high as possible on funeral scaffolds. In an age when we fly at 30,000 feet and even the most banal cell phone chatter bounces off of satellites 22,000 miles into space, we have lost the sense of what heights formerly meant: liminal spots of land, places where the realm of earth encounters the realm of what's above.

As spatial creatures, we necessarily live in the in between places. Unlike birds or fish or drifting pollen spores, we need to spend our days with our feet on the ground, negotiating the horizontal plane we call home. It must be almost a universal childhood experience to lie on your back and imagine falling into the endless fathoms of air. I suspect that such a fantasy of entry into the realm of what's above shapes us in ways we cannot fully understand, and, further, that the knowledge we lie at the very bottom of an atmosphere somehow lurks in the back of our spiritual imaginations. There is a reason angels have always been drawn with wings.

As I walk around at Acacia Cemetery—which like any cemetery, constitutes a place specifically designated to return our bodies to the earth— it strikes me how persistently this is a place drawn to altitude. Ever since the cemetery opened, a flagpole has stood on the brow of Pilot Knob, and the finial ornament atop the pole is a bronze American eagle that faces east, wings open and ready to take off. When I first noticed that metal eagle, I thought it was a richly political statement: on the sacred grounds of the Sioux, the American nation erected a flag and its national emblem looking back to the lands from which the white man came. On the other hand, the real significance of that eagle may not be the way it announces a new political order but, rather, the way it declares a continuity with the old: at the top of a sacred hill, we still wish to go higher, to nudge just a shade more toward the unreachable region of altitude.

The burial practice of the Sioux—to which H. C. Yarrow, in an 1878 ethnographic report to the Smithsonian Institution, gave the charmingly funky term "aerial sepulture"—was explained by such early ethnographers of the Dakota as the missionary brothers Gideon and Samuel Pond as a pragmatic matter, arising from the long spans when the ground was frozen. Never mind that the practice was conducted year 'round, or that the remains of the Indian deceased, were in fact, customarily buried after two weeks.

A record of these funeral scaffolds survives in the sketches of Seth Eastman, an army officer who served at Fort Snelling directly across the river. Eastman was a Maine Yankee who graduated from West Point in 1829. A skilled artist (he later wrote a textbook, *Treatise on Topography*, for military draftsmen that was used in the service academies until it was made obsolete by photography), Eastman realized that his postings on the frontier allowed him to watch a different sort of sunset—the last moments of a native culture as it crumbled.

He went wherever the army told him to go—Texas, Florida, back to West Point, to the Arkansas frontier—but the artist in him understood his best shot at posterity lay in his record of the Mdewakanton Sioux. During two tours of duty in Minnesota, Eastman sketched and painted Indian life with photographic accuracy. Eventually he was chosen to contribute more than three hundred plates to Henry Schoolcraft's magisterial work published by the Office of Indian Affairs, *Indian Tribes of the United States*. Eastman had another sort of posterity bound up with the Sioux; in 1831 he married a woman named Stands Sacred in a Sioux ceremony, fathered a child by her, and then left them both when he was transferred to Texas. When he returned in 1841, he brought along a new white wife from New England. A recent biography, *Painting the Dakota*, relates the story of his abandonment with surprising detachment and forgiveness. Evidently, in the long view, history judges Eastman by his paintings.

He painted several pictures of funeral scaffolds: at least one, which is now at the Peabody Museum of Anthropology at Harvard, is believed to be of Pilot Knob. Another is in the United States Capitol. Several times I have brought a volume of his paintings with me when I visit Acacia Park, and I am struck by how readily the landforms can be recognized. In the painting from the Peabody Museum, a group of six Indians are gathered in front of a structure about seven feet high. It is a frame made of tree branches, topped by a platform on which a board coffin rests. One of the standing Indians is bare to the waist and holding a ribbon. The body has clearly been placed on its scaffold in a process of formalized mourning. Four are seated on the ground, two cutting ritual scars into their forearms and another cutting his hair in grief. A bucket for food or water hangs from a horizontal pole. Most important, even the rude structure serves literally a lofty purpose; one of the upright logs is much taller than the others. A pennant flies from this highest pole, above the coffin.

One evening in early April I sat on the granite bench at the western rim of Pilot Knob, and looked across at the airport. It was starting to get chilly, but I was reluctant to leave. That's often a busy time for the airport, but on this particular night there were no jets coming or going. The edge of the hill drops off sharply on that side, and I watched the sunlight pour over the expanse of quiet gravesites, each day sinking nearer to disappearance below, and thought about the funeral scaffolds that had once stood precisely where I sat.

I started to wonder just how absent the Indians of 150 years ago really were, how fully they had been erased from the landscape. I wondered if, at the very least, the Sioux in Eastman's paintings were any more absent than dozens, or a hundred, or a thousand, of the modern burials on whose graves I had just walked. We all experience instances when we sense an impulse to memory rising within us, but when the thread that joins us to the vast particularity of the past has been severed: the faces in the tintypes, the strangers' names on a gravestone, the nameless Indians weeping below a nameless coffin in Eastman's meticulous watercolor. In the brackish zones where memory has become irretrievable, it may be only the power of place that can step in to sacralize our experience.

I don't want to see Pilot Knob opened for town homes and commercial developments. We need quiet places. One of the reasons we need uncluttered and open spaces is the simple fact that in such places, other sorts of thought are possible. The artist and cartographer Tim Robinson employs the term "geophany" to describe those moments when our awareness of the earth imparts a meaning to what we apprehend, a meaning that arises somewhere before or after language.

And we need cemeteries—peaceful cemeteries—in particular, because when we walk near the dead we are in some faint way resisting the great facelessness of modern life, the homogenization of our consciousness worked by the "mass cult" of advertising, fashion, movies, and all the relentless levelers of our time.

I thought about these things while I looked out over a broad and carefully landscaped apron of lawn. The top branches of still bare maple trees were at eye level, etched black against the setting sun. Dozens of birds perched in the maples, and though I could not identify them—waxwings perhaps, or spring warblers—I could see them make brief sorties up and back from the highest branches, and then return as if on a tether. As night gathered, they continued to rise and stab at the sky.

REVISITING OAK HILL

Nights when worms came up
from the saturated earth to breathe,
my brother and I brought coffee cans
and flashlights to this cemetery slope.
We would sweep our feeble beams
over the damp grass, looking for fat
nightcrawlers drawn out like naked veins,
and at a touch their forms became
snatched-away ropes—tissue slipping
through our fingers like water down a drain.

When I was twenty-one, we buried my father
a hundred yards farther up this hill.
After he'd died, I could not imagine
that a day would come when I might stand
beside his grave and not weep,
but thirty years later, I can:
though nothing, nothing, nothing
has been forgotten. Today I remember
sobbing for my father. Today I remember
catching nightcrawlers in the rain.

OCEAN-GOING BIRD

(for Jim Flannery)

At day's end we stand admiring
the painting you bought in Ireland:
solitary bird, an albatross or shearwater,
a pelagic icon soaring over
the sea's unfathomable blue-black skin.
For such birds, I have heard, time
is a fourth and knowable dimension.
In oceanic glide, they move knowing
the hours in their feathers and frame,
cartilage keeping the days as if it were a mind.
Which is how we know the world, too:
heart mysteries in our pulsing hearts.
Today we walked amid six generations
of Atlanta's dead, some forgotten,
others recalled with pomp and great to-do.
Walking together on the red brick lanes
of Oakland Cemetery, held
in the crystal net of years and days,
a silence overtook the afternoon.
We moved among and above each passing name.

LOOKING FOR PATRICK

Rochester, Minnesota, always turns up on the various short lists of America's most livable cities, and the Mayo Clinic and its hospitals have made the city world famous. But when I think of Rochester, I am more likely to think of it as the burial place of Patrick Cudmore, a pathetic and long-forgotten Irish littérateur who has captured my interest on and off for more than twenty years. I also think of the flock of 30,000 Canada geese that winters at Silver Lake in Rochester, a wide spot behind a dam on the Zumbro River. In recent years the city's public health officials have grown worried about the enormous quantities of waste matter the geese leave all over town, and the city that formerly put a Canada goose on its official stationery is now trying to discourage their presence.

Cudmore lies immediately east of that goose-crowded lake, in a Catholic burial ground called Calvary Cemetery. In the autumn, rafts of geese take flight from Silver Lake to scavenge in the corn stubble and sloughs of the surrounding countryside. They fly over Cudmore's grave, and, because I know that he was an immigrant Irishman himself, it is tempting to think of their flight as somehow emblematic of the Wild Geese of Irish romance, those exiled aristocrats whose descendants found glory in the armies and palaces of Europe.

No doubt Cudmore himself would have liked to make that connection. But, as any serious writer knows, you have to be careful about pushing a metaphor too far. Cudmore made his home, not in the eighteenth-century courts of France and Spain but in the muddy prairie towns of nineteenth-century America, and the geese that pass over Calvary Cemetery may be beautiful and graceful when they fly in formation, but their comings and goings are attended by a great clatter, all of it pointless, and homeowners near the lake complain that the honking, hissing waterfowl spread their green droppings on every lawn.

Patrick Cudmore was born in County Limerick, Ireland, in 1831. He died in Minneapolis in 1916. His gravestone declares to posterity that he was a "poet, author, and historian" and perhaps, in some senses, he was. The gravestone makes no claim about his competence at any of these professions.

In 1898, Cudmore published an odd little six-page *Autobiography* with the firm of P. J. Kenedy in New York, the most prominent Catholic publishing house in its time. It is hard to imagine who might have bought a copy. Yet if there is any quality that distinguished Cudmore, it was his conviction that history would take note of him. Like Stephen Dedalus's father, he was a praiser of his own past, though Cudmore was also a praiser of his own future. As a schoolboy, he recalls, "I quit all kinds of amusements and devoted myself exclusively to study. I frequently met boys after school to debate the history of Greece, Rome, England and Ireland . . . I resolved on making a mark in the world and perpetuating my name. I prided myself on being *faber sum fortuna* and *primus inter pares*. I had high aspirations, towering ambition, love of honor, glory, and fame. I did not like the idea of dying 'unknown, unhonored, and unsung'—to be forgotten like the worm of the earth! I dreaded oblivion! Something seemed to inspire me with the thought of future honor and fame."

He first aspired to be a sea captain. Then an astronomer. Then a priest. Aspiration was as much a part of Cudmore's make-up as a limp or a scar might be for another man. Cudmore personally donated copies of his books to the Minnesota Historical Society. A review from the *Manchester Guardian* was pasted onto the inside cover of Cudmore's *Prophecy of the Twentieth Century: the Twentieth Century*: it described the long poem as "Curious and incoherent . . . in irregular rhymed couplets." Almost certainly, the author had personally mailed his book off to Manchester, and cherished the snub—his logic being that going without honor obliquely confirmed that he was, indeed, a prophet.

Cudmore first hove into my life in the summer of 1976, when I thought I might undertake to write a history of the Irish in Minnesota. Cudmore's grandiosity may be why I was drawn to him: in 1976, I had not had one minute of training in research or historiography; in fact, I had never taken a college-level history course.

But I had fun that summer, sifting through the scant literature on the topic collected at the Minnesota Historical Society, among which were

Cudmore's books. Anyone who undertakes serious archival research knows the special frisson of excitement that comes on unearthing some fact that no one else in the world has known, or has wanted to know. Cudmore has provided that frisson, for me. At first, I thought I had found in him some sort of rustic original, a wannabe Robert Burns in Minnesota. But when I actually read his works, I found that he brought no ability to his aspiration. Decades later—having become something of an authority on Irish-American literature—I realize, too, that I cannot hold him as a particular exemplar of any sort of literary tradition. Writing and versifying was a participatory sport in the nineteenth century; every small town had its dabbler in verse, its resident controversialist. Yet Cudmore's heroic misjudgment about his own significance continued to interest me long after I realized that he was, to all intents, a nonentity—one who fervently denied his own nullity, but a nonentity all the same.

Once, I made a photocopy of Cudmore's portrait (it appears in the 1899 *Cudmore's Prophecy of the Twentieth Century*) and showed it to acquaintances, asking them to guess at the personality of the man in the picture. I got answers like these: "He looks intelligent, and a little bit playful." "He looks smart but rigid." "He looks religious, and also very intelligent." "He looks intelligent but stern." "The wrinkle in his brow suggests that he's intelligent." "He looks like a paranoid genius."

Cudmore was intelligent. As a young man in New York, he attended anatomy lectures at Bellevue Hospital. He took a course of lectures (about what, he does not say) at the Cooper Institute. It was probably there that he earned a Bachelor of Humanities degree; he always added the letters B.H. after his name. He studied law at an unspecified law school. To pass the bar, he "read law," as Abe Lincoln did. He absorbed constitutional history. He studied the histories of the Jews, Romans, English, Scotch, French, and Germans. Late in life, he took up Spanish.

Like many autodidacts, he retained a profound sense of ownership about his learning. The titles of his books tell as much: *Cudmore's Constitutional History, Cudmore's Poems and Songs, Cudmore's Battle of Clontarf and Other Poems, Cudmore's Prophecy of the Twentieth Century.*

Cudmore spent three years in the US Army. His recollections of these years read as one long string of occasions when he was snubbed and cheated by the military brass. After failing to find enough trusting volunteers in Rice and Steele counties to make up an Irish regiment—with himself as captain—Cudmore's squad was combined with a larger squad from St. Paul to form the Tenth Regiment of Minnesota. The unit was to elect its own officers. Cudmore explains that two brothers-in-law named Sullivan leagued against him to skew the voting.

Then the Tenth Regiment was sent west to fight the Indians. There, Cudmore grew embittered when a "Know-Nothing" Colonel Baker passed him over for promotion. After driving the Indians across the Missouri River, he reports "Major Cook told me that if I would give Colonel Baker a good puff in the newspapers he would make me a company sergeant. I refused to puff such a dishonorable man . . . I was too proud to stoop and cringe to such a man, and preferred to remain a private in the ranks."

Cudmore was sent south to fight in the Civil War in 1862, where he recounts that he was once again cheated out of an officer's commission. He injured his spine in the Battle of Tupelo. He became so sick with diarrhea that he had to be sent to the military hospital in Memphis. Almost a third of the *Autobiography* is given over to Cudmore's account of his military career. He paints himself as more a victim than a hero; nevertheless, he never got any closer to heroism.

It astounds me that no reference to the Irish famine appears in the *Autobiography*; Cudmore had left Ireland in 1846, the second year of the Great Potato Famine that would eventually starve a million Irish people and displace another million. But Patrick wrote his life as if it were history that ought to be paying attention to him.

For most people, marriage and family warrant mention in an autobiography, too. Not for Patrick. Some time after he arrived in New York, Cudmore married a woman named Mary Anne Lynch. He allots her a total of five sentences. "My wife was a few years my senior. She was sensible and economical. She could save the dollars and the cents. I made her cashier and treasurer, which left my mind free from the cares of 'pater familias' and gave me ample time for study." In 1857, Cudmore's wife died. This event, he comments, "broke up all my calculations."

Succinct, but it surpasses the attention he gives his heirs. Not until the end of his *Autobiography* does he almost inadvertently drop the fact that he has a child: "July, 1895, I published a new book of poems entitled 'Battle of Clontarf and Other Poems.' I am now the author of five books. I am preparing a book on Ireland, including the civil government of Ireland. I have a son, Daniel John Cudmore, living at Rochester, Minn, who has a family of one son and two daughters, William, Nellie, and Mary. I donated copies of 'The Irish Republic,' 'Constitutional History,' 'Poems,' 'Buchanan's Conspiracy,' and 'The Battle of Clontarf' to the principal libraries of the world."

Surely, the barely mentioned son understood where he stood in the eyes of his father: somewhere well below those books launched at the principal libraries of the world.

But I have never found any of Patrick's descendants. On the internet, I looked for persons named Cudmore in Minnesota. A directory of residential listings turns up almost a dozen, but I have a hard time reaching any of them. A number in the western part of the state has been disconnected. I reach a woman in northern Minnesota; she is now separated from her husband, whose name it is, and she declines to give me his new number. Another woman in Duluth believes I am a telemarketer, warns me not to call back, then hangs up.

Eventually I reach a man named Dan Cudmore, in Clements, Minnesota, and because the *Autobiography* mentioned the son was named Daniel I am hoping this man will be a descendant. But his family is from Texas, and before that, Prince Edward Island. He's interested in Patrick's story, though certain they are unrelated. In time I make contact with Cudmores on both coasts. All of their families have routed through the maritime provinces. None is related to Patrick. I sent photocopies of the *Autobiography* off to several, and they are interested. Raymond Cudmore, an energetic family historian in Washington, D.C., had seen it at the library of Catholic University—another of those principal libraries of the world, no doubt. After reading Patrick's memoir, Mrs. Erwin Cudmore, an eighty-year-old woman in Park River, North Dakota, sends me an e-mail to say she is glad his traits don't seem to have been passed on.

Kilfinane, the town in Limerick where Cudmore was born, is also the hometown of an Irish poet whom I know slightly, Gabriel Rosenstock. I sent Gabriel an e-mail to ask him if he knows whether Cudmore's name survived in any sort of communal or folk memory. He hadn't, in his recollection, but he put me in touch with Mannix Joyce, a longtime expert on local history who writes for *The Limerick Leader*. I mailed off a letter, a photocopy of the six-page autobiography, and samples of Cudmore's poetry to Joyce.

Joyce had never heard of him or the name. For a man inordinately concerned with his own posterity, Patrick seems to have vanished from memory. But Cudmore never thought he would be forgotten. The poet Horace wrote that his work would be "a monument more lasting than bronze," and Cudmore, who set out to become an author after his military career ended, had similar confidence. His near-total lack of literary talent seems not to have occurred to him.

In prose, Patrick didn't so much write books as fill them up. He spewed polemic, calling on evidence with the subtlety of a looter filling a gunnysack. Among the topics he treats in his 1896 book *Cleveland's Maladministration, Free Trade, Protection and Reciprocity* are the history of Irish republicanism, with special attention to the doomed campaigns of Wolfe Tone; the necessity of a Nicaraguan canal to link the Atlantic and Pacific; detailed reportage on the world's wheat harvest; and the legitimacy of the Hawaiian royal family.

He also believed himself to be a poet. In 1885, he published *The Le Sueur Litany*, a 146-line rhyming malediction against Michael Doran, an Irish-born state senator living in Le Sueur, Minnesota:

> Where Doran will go th' fiend can tell—
> He emigrated from back of Kells—
> He came over in a rotten ship;
> Cursed be that hulk that did not sink.

There is something exuberantly over-the-top about these fulminations:

> May poisonous serpents with their stings
> Pierce the flesh of the Le Sueur Rings . . .

> May all rheums their filthy bodies hack
> Until their bone in their sockets crack—
> May plagues and rust take Doran's wheat,
> May his corn be burnt by frost and sleet . . .

Doran attained national prominence as a Bourbon Democrat, a part of the political machine that secured a presidential nomination for Grover Cleveland. After several unsuccessful runs at office after coming to Minnesota, Cudmore had been elected to one term as Le Sueur county attorney. But by the time he wrote this, he had not held elected office in twenty years.

Yet Cudmore cast himself as a feared Irish bard of legend, whose satires could chase a prince into exile. In an 1884 verse titled "The Poet" he declares, "the bard when rich or independent poor / No mercy shows to the churlish boor." One of Cudmore's verses takes aim at President Chester Arthur; it is titled, with characteristic subtlety, "Arthur is a Flunkey."

Every writer—every thoughtful writer, anyway—knows that he's continually placing bets that history will remember what he writes; to put it in deep, psychoanalytic terms, he is manipulating symbols against the body. The other thing that any thoughtful writer knows is that it won't work. A book won't hold back death, no more than lighting a candle will keep dark from falling.

And yet, at least twice in my life, I've been drawn to study scribblers who think they can blather their way into posterity. My final project for my M.A. in English was an essay about the book *Joe Gould's Secret*, in which an unstable man named Joe Gould claimed to be writing an ambitious "oral history of the world." He told his biographer Joseph Mitchell that "A couple of generations after I'm dead and gone . . . the Ph.D.s will start lousing through my work. Just imagine their surprise. 'Why, I be damned,' they'll say, 'this fellow was the most brilliant historian of the century.' They'll give me my due."

Gould was a Harvard graduate. He never actually wrote more than a few pages of the book he claimed was going to do him honor for all time. He died in the Pilgrim State Hospital for the insane. At a certain point it occurs to me that Cudmore was a lot like Gould. At a certain point, it occurs to me, too, that between the two of them I have spent a great deal of my time and energy trying to understand deranged men who pinned their hopes for immortality on the written word.

I am not sure I want to scratch any further.

I've met too many Irishmen like Cudmore—outspoken men who insist on addressing "the issues." They have a talent for being instantly right, and clamp onto opinions like a pit bull onto a leg. They write letters to the editor and clip them for scrapbooks. They wear cowboy hats to city council meetings and to scholarly conferences. Cudmore recalls proudly a time when, "One Brown, editor of the *Faribault Central Republican*, assailed me in his newspaper. I wrote two articles or letters against him in the *Faribault Statesman*, and completely shut him up."

Did he shut him up? Or did Brown prudently decide, Why bother? From a distance of more than a hundred years, it's easy to infer that at a certain point, Cudmore crossed the line into looniness. To disagree with him was to invite calumny and abuse; if anyone declined to debate him, he interpreted it to mean they had been cowed. The more he ranted, the more irrelevant he became.

I would need to be a better theologian or church historian to articulate it, but I am convinced there is a distinctly Irish spiritual failing, to which Cudmore fell victim—a heresy that implicitly believes it's the personality which is immortal. Frank McCourt's absent father, out performing nightly for the barflies of Limerick; Joyce's "character" father; Yeats's posturing; Cudmore picking fights in the letters columns of small-town newspapers.

Sitting in the reading room of the Historical Society with a copy of the *Prophecy*, I imagine Cudmore having fallen into the conviction that he was a singular genius, a man about whom others talked.

I also realize that in most ways, Cudmore is a bore.

From my office, I check the website of the Minnesota Historical Society and find a link I had not seen before: DEATH CERTIFICATES. I type the name Patrick Cudmore and the year 1916 and am brought to a page with his death certificate number.

That night I visit the MHS library and learn that the certificates are all on microfilm. The microfilm room holds information, holds facts, the way the night sky holds stars. Case after case of drawers line its perimeter, each containing dozens of drawers, each in turn containing hundreds of rolls of film. The drawers slide out on silent ball bearings, like doors to secret passageways in the old movies. But they are not secret: if you know where to look, you can confidently skate your way through the baffling number of records. A helpful staff person loads the film directly on a machine equipped with a printer. She loops one end of the film around the take-up spool; within a minute, I have Patrick's record in front of me. He died February 14, 1916, at the Soldiers' Home in Minneapolis, where he had lived eight years. His father was also named Patrick Cudmore, his mother Katherine Monahan. The cause of death was arteriosclerosis. The body was taken to Rochester, Minnesota, for burial.

The Old Soldier's Home still stands, about three miles from my back door. That coincidence impresses me, but more impressive is the simple fact that I have located this record with practically no effort.

The Rochester *Daily Post and Record* is easily found, and on February 15 it notes, "Word has reached Rochester concerning the death of P. Cudmore, father of John Cudmore of this city in Minneapolis Monday afternoon. Mr. Cudmore was at the bedside when the elderly Mr. Cudmore passed away. The remains will be brought to Rochester this evening and funeral services will probably be held at 9 o'clock Thursday morning at St. John's Catholic Church."

Word has reached Rochester. . . . Patrick would have liked that. European and Asiatic papers please copy.

On February 17 the *Daily Post and Record* notes the funeral that morning, observing that the pall bearers were James Conway, M. Madden, John Madden, Barney Heaton, and Robert Morrison.

I walk across the hall to the main reading room of the historical society, where I enter "St. John's Catholic Church Rochester" in the electronic catalog. It turns out that in 1989, the cemetery committee of the Olmsted County Historical Society compiled a detailed listing of cemetery inscriptions. An inventory of St. John's Cemetery forms the sixth volume.

At this point, I begin to think, *This is too easy: I've been in the library only a half an hour and know exactly what I came to find out.* But I request the cemetery register, and when it comes, turn to the index. One Cudmore, on page 76: in row 41, plot 18, is a stone that reads:

<blockquote>
P Cudmore, B. H. b. June 24 1831, d,. Feb 14 1916
born in Morestown Parish of Kilfinane Co of Limerick Ireland.
Poet, Historian & Author of 7 books, soldier in Co H 1ot Regt
MN Vol of Civil War of 1861.
</blockquote>

It's too easy, I think again, and then I realize that it's not too easy. It's just a matter of having looked for Patrick in the first age in history when vast library collections with online catalogs, the internet, interlibrary loans, and telecommunications can retrieve the life, and life work, of someone as obscure as Cudmore.

And then I realized something else: that ever since I began to look for Patrick, I had been scripting the story all along in preparation for what a poet friend calls "a planned epiphany." I had been setting up in my mind a scenario where either Cudmore had vanished, or—in what I had imagined would be the better story—I found his gravestone in the midst of an Ozymandias-like desolation. Instead, I now knew that I could drive to the corner of 11th Avenue and Fifth Street NE in Rochester and walk to his burial site.

I was begrudging him the attainment of his fondest wish, to have dodged oblivion. Then again, maybe oblivion isn't what it used to be; historical forgetfulness has become more complex. Once, a modest life could be predictably lost to history, after a few generations, and that inevitability served as a humbling, oddly reassuring certainty. Today, the comforting erosion of memory can be halted—though the vast majority of fact stored in our databases may prove, in the end, to be no more significant than the millions of aluminum beer cans that will outlast the pyramids.

The Minnesota Historical Society scrupulously protects its holdings, and just as scrupulously observes copyright law. To have photocopies made, I need to turn the book back to the library's service desk and to read and to sign several disclaimers. Waiting for the copies to come back, I browsed through magazines in the reading room, and in one—the Winter, 2002, issue of *History News*—I chanced on an article about the business and historical records that were lost in the attacks on the World Trade Center on September 11.

Accompanying the article was a picture of a New York City fireman walking among the eighteenth-century headstones in Trinity churchyard, ankle-deep in documents that had drifted there following the towers' collapse.

Sheets of paper, millions of words covering the dead, documents falling like silt to the bottom of a river; in some way I connected the picture in the magazine to the fact that I had found Patrick. The photograph stays in my imagination, like a parable whose meaning will not come clear.

Not long after this, on a warm July morning, I drove to Rochester.

I had a sort of vague idea I might be able to meet a long-distant first cousin for lunch. His father, my uncle, had managed the American Legion Club in Rochester years ago, and used to send me autographs he'd collected from celebrities who'd come in while visiting the Mayo Clinic. I could not find his name in any directories, though, and my mother hadn't heard from him in a decade. I recognized the irony: I was going to visit a grave and do research on a man and family whom I'd never met, while I couldn't make connections with my own living relatives.

But at least in Patrick's case, I knew where he was.

The staff at the Olmsted County Historical Society library, like all library staff, were professional and obliging. They asked me what I wanted to learn, and I had to admit that I wasn't sure: "Whatever you have on the Cudmores," I said. It seemed to me that someday I'd like to somehow track down one of Patrick's descendants, to learn whether this man who cared so much about his atrocious literary posterity, was remembered with any affection at all by the descendants he had—despite his indifference—left behind.

In the city directory I learned that Cudmore's son Daniel John was a blacksmith at the time of his father's death; a sheet of their stationery in the business file advertised horse shoeing and plow repairs. The historical society had helpfully indexed all of the obituaries in the *Rochester Post Bulletin*. Daniel's older son, William, worked with him at the forge, then became fire chief in 1919, and a history of the fire department noted that he gained a reputation for being a demanding commander who forced his volunteers to get up at 5:00 A.M. for training exercises. That stern regime sounded like the grandfather.

Another of Patrick's grandsons was a high school football star. A librarian pulled the probate file for Daniel John Cudmore, which was completed in 1944, twenty years after his death. At that point, Daniel's widow,

Catherine, was living in Los Angeles. The three surviving grandchildren had scattered to Vancouver, Canada, to Benton Harbor, Michigan, and to Pierre, South Dakota. (Eventually, an online telephone directory led me to a Rodney Cudmore living in Pierre, but when I reached him, he knew only that the Cudmores who used to live there had moved away, and were not related.)

I wrote down the names of the descendants, and searched microfilm to find the obituaries, all of which opened with the familiar formula: "Word has reached Rochester that ____ Cudmore, formerly of this city, has died . . ."

Calvary is a large, well-groomed burial ground owned by the Catholic diocese of Winona, Minnesota; the caretaker, whom I happened to meet as I walked in, told me that it's still used for about a hundred interments a year. It is a well-visited place, too. I saw a mother and her young daughter ride in on bicycles and place flowers, and a woman who was talking aloud at the grave of a Korean War veteran, who quieted down when she saw me.

The caretaker was shoveling ornamental rock off the back of a flatbed truck, to spread around a grove of arbor vitae at the entrance. He said if I needed help I should ask him, or flag down the kid on the lawn tractor. I told him I thought I could find the site I was looking for because I had the details from the cemetery inscription book.

I began walking the grounds. They are neat and well maintained—a little too much so. With trees and shrubs over-trimmed in a Louis XIV fashion, they reminded me of the set of *Edward Scissorhands*. Touches of middlebrow Catholic taste crop up everywhere: plastic flowers, a gravestone with four-leafed clovers alongside the Irish name, and an ostentatious monument with a carved fetus on it, put up by the Knights of Columbus in memory of the unborn. One Catholic touch that is dignified and moving, though, is a large section in the middle of the cemetery reserved for the graves of Franciscan nuns, in orderly rows of simple identical headstones. It struck me that their simplicity reflected something deeply religious, and that Patrick's self-congratulatory epitaph—which I had not yet seen—was actually quite out of place in a Catholic cemetery. In Catholic cemeteries, there seems to be a protocol that conveys it is all very well to record the dates of your birth and death, and maybe even your whereabouts when these events happened—but don't go announcing your individuality in stone.

My directions proved useless, and after a half-hour of trying to count off the plot and row numbers I realized I'd better ask for help. I could hear the rhythmic sound of the caretaker, shoveling away in the corner; the young man on the lawn mower was driving away from me, but when he doubled back I caught his eye and waved at him. He took his ear protectors off and we walked to the maintenance shed, where he pulled out a single volume and with a few flips of the page located Cudmore's entry at Section 9, Lot 9—not even close to the record in the book I had consulted. I learned something new: Cudmore's son Daniel, and daughter-in-law, Catherine, had been assigned plots, though I knew from the obituary that Catherine was buried on the West Coast. But Daniel, whose obituary I had not found, was buried alongside his father.

I walked directly to Section 9 and found Cudmore's grave in minutes.

Patrick's resting place is marked by a substantial stone of polished gray granite, on a sandstone plinth. It stands almost five feet high. A cross, with I.H.S. in a medallion at its center, is carved on the front, with tracery of ailanthus leaves and another sort of sculpted vegetation that I didn't recognize. The name Cudmore is written in ten-inch letters across the front on the monument.

The biographical inscription is written on the reverse of the stone, in capital letters. Below it, there was a verse not recorded in the book of cemetery inscriptions, a couplet that has to have been written by Cudmore himself. "Disturb Not My Bones Or Clay / Let Me Sleep Till Judgment Day." Like Shakespeare, Patrick had left the world with doggerel on his tombstone.

It was not the showiest monument in this part of the cemetery: still, someone—perhaps Cudmore himself, who clearly composed his own epitaph, or perhaps his son, in an unexpected gesture of filial devotion—had spent hundreds of 1916 dollars on this marker. If the latter, Daniel's thanks was to have his name left off of Patrick's headstone.

And I suppose the proper thing to do, when you visit someone's grave, is to stop and offer a prayer, or, if you believe as I do, that at least part of the reason we have cemeteries is to remind us that Ecclesiastes was right and that all things do pass, to wait for the place itself to speak a prayer.

But I didn't do anything so solemn. What I did was take out a disposable camera and snap a few pictures.

No prayers came, and for that, I blame Patrick. I blame him for the surfeit of self he'd intruded on the world. I thought back to the family history I had retrieved that morning, which indicated that this once fairly prominent Rochester family had dispersed in short order; and, though I had nothing firm on which to base the intuition, I wondered if there wasn't something obscurely sad in the reasons why—something that led back to the grandfather's conviction of his own greatness.

I thought of him as a laughably bad poet, yet there had come a point when I stopped laughing. To Patrick, his wife was a bookkeeper; his son, a footnote. He squandered his intelligence on petty snubs and peevishness. He had demanded immortality without stopping to cultivate talent. Even in death he filled the space around him with his ego, and as I walked to my car, I began to understand that there was a lot to forget about Patrick Cudmore.

NEAR PLAINVIEW

On a day colder than it ought to have been,
we diverted down a county road
and pulled over to one side. There
we walked among the hand-set
stone foundation of a farmhouse,
now open to the sky and filling in with
sheet metal, ragweed stalks
and tallus. Then we crossed

to the Pleasant Prairie graveyard,
a place of plastic flowers,
too-blue and too-pink in the April snow.
No matter. What I remember is this:
that near the back fence, a loop
of barbed-wire—I'd say eighty
or a hundred feet—hung on a post,
its wire thorns rusted into a crude letter O,
a wreath left in the rain long years.

OLD ST. VINCENT'S, HOUSTON

The parish now locks the gates
against boys with spray paint,
boys with too much liquor,
boys on dirt bikes, all the empty
mischiefs that hate a cemetery,
but the priest who answers our knock
shows us in gladly, pointing
with pride to his roses
in the graveyard corner,
heavy with pastel blooms.

My guide knows the stories
below us: the Civil War hero
whose grave was lost and found;
his merchant son-in-law,
whose family's still in business
at the mall; the milliner
who adopted two sons
as a widow, and died rich
in spite of her reckless charity;
thirteen-year-old Fritz, who died
in a seminary: at his stone
I wonder aloud, *Sweet Jesus,*
what sort of life was that?

It has to be a source
of gladness that roses grow
here now, behind a fence,
across from the glass-
littered basketball courts
of a housing project.
The shadeless towers
of Houston loom a mile away.
Thank God for rosebeds.
Oh, by all means, rejoice.

THE OLD ORDER

Fortunate country, that is one day to receive hearts like Alexandra's into its bosom, to give them out again in the yellow wheat, in the rustling corn, in the shining eyes of youth!

WILLA CATHER, *O PIONEERS!*

One warm, dry summer afternoon—it was an August first—I impulsively took a day off work in order to ride along with a friend who had a day's business in Worthington, in far southwestern Minnesota. I always enjoy the countryside in high summer. As we drove down highways 169 and 60, hay balers and other farm machinery were busy working the fields, one of the most calming sights I know. This particular day came at that moment of summer when tones of brown and gold first begin to seep into the lavishly green landscape, a quiet turning point when the knowledge that harvest-time is imminent comes over us like an instinct.

Still, as pleasant as the ride was, I was not quite sure how I would pass the afternoon once we arrived in Worthington, where I knew not a living soul. Then it occurred to me that as I had several hours and my friend's car at my disposal, one way to pass it would be to indulge my interest in country graveyards.

I had the good luck, too, to find the Nobles County Historical Society open, and to meet its part-time director, Mrs. Roxann Polzine. Like every librarian and small-town historian I have ever met, she was immensely helpful. When I told her of my plans, she went directly to a file cabinet and pulled out a bundle of clippings that dealt with burial grounds in the area, and on a county map she plotted a circuit that would lead me to cemeteries in the small towns of St. Kilian, Lismore, Adrian, and Rushmore. But the site that she most recommended I visit was an abandoned Amish cemetery near Wilmont, Minnesota. All she could tell me was that it was "a very interesting place." I am glad that I took her advice.

Nobles County lies near the Iowa line. Lines mean more on the prairies than they do elsewhere; township lines, 640-acre sections, county boundaries with corners inscribe this area. Nobles County is also the windiest part of the state. The wind blew before the land was charted and pays no attention to any map, and it blows here still. One of the largest energy-producing wind farms in the upper Midwest lies about ten miles away, at Buffalo Ridge; the out-of-state energy company that operates it reports impressive numbers about how much wind-generated electricity it is able to sell "back into the grid." In 2002, a lone windmill was put up only a half-mile from the cemetery. It is 235 feet high and painted a pale blue. Its three blades turn quietly and purposefully all day long. There is something faintly mysterious about their revolutions, which are utterly predictable but nonetheless fascinating to watch.

The cemetery is a rectangle of bare earth, surveyed at twenty-six-and-a-half feet by sixteen-and-a-half feet. It is notched into the southeast corner of a sixty-acre cornfield owned and farmed by Michael Remakel, whose family has farmed here for eighty-five years. Because it is unfenced, and uncared for, the boundaries of the Amish cemetery are slightly more ragged than one expects in this landscape of straight lines. A closely mowed right-of-way forms a swale that dips between the roads and the cemetery, then rises to the edge of the cornfield. Weeds persist and spread everywhere across the ground, right up to the edge of the burial ground. Weeds don't grow in the cemetery—not because of any care it has received but because the yearly herbicidal application applied to the cornfield includes this corner in its sweep. Walls of corn frame the burial site on two sides. I calculated that the space of the cemetery displaces sixty-six stalks.

No memorial stones mark the place. Newspaper stories in the file at the Nobles County Historical Society quote the memories of an older resident who recalled seeing tumbling wooden crosses and sunken graves at the Amish Cemetery. But that was seventy years ago; they have long vanished into the earth, as have the twenty-six Amish farmers buried here. Lately, Roxann Polzine has begun ferreting out the names of those settlers from county death records. She has retrieved eight names, thus far.

A field of soybeans lies immediately east of the site; otherwise, the surrounding land is given over to corn. Three roads meet nearby: a gravel road, State Highway 266, and a paved east-west county road. The place cannot be recognized as a cemetery from any of these thoroughfares. However, in 1950—at the request of descendants who lived out-of-state and who feared that soon no one would be left who could recall that human remains were interred there—county officials marked it with a flat block of granite bearing the two words "Amish Cemetery."

A 1986 book by David Luthy, *The Amish in America: Settlements That Failed*—a state-by-state compendium of frustration and defeat among these modest people—states that the Amish settlement near Wilmont lasted only nineteen years, and that it was a divided community for most of that time. Starting in 1891, Old Order Amish, those who strictly observe the group's highly prescribed traditions, began to arrive from Ontario. They were soon followed by more progressive Mennonites. By 1910, all had departed for Michigan and Indiana, or had gone back to Canada. Although their farms had prospered, the community fell apart under an irreconcilable conflict between the two groups about the proper place for worship. When the Mennonites proposed building a meeting-house instead of holding worship services in homes, the Old Order Amish broke from the community. A building would have violated the spirit of *gellasenheit*—a radical resistance to self-importance—that binds together Amish society.

A recent rain had left pockmarks on the rectangle of baked earth where the Amish lay in unmarked graves. The next rain will wash those pockmarks away. It was hard not to conclude that the more humble Amish had had their way, indeed.

Amish life could hardly be more remote from my own background, and most of what I know about the group comes from recent reading in books with such titles as *A Peculiar People, The Riddle of Amish Culture,* and *On the Backroad to Heaven.* I'm a Catholic by birth and by practice, though a particular stripe of Catholic, to be sure; one of those self-mocking, post-Vatican II Irish Americans for whom religion is important, but for whom irony is as much a badge of identity as rosary beads were for our grandparents. But a few months before I visited this cemetery, I met an Amish man named Johann on an Amtrak train crossing Wisconsin, with whom I had a memorable conversation. I was glad when he sat down next to me in the observation car. I am about to turn fifty and have lived all of my life in the Midwest; should it surprise me that I've met hundreds of Buddhists, hundreds of Hindus, but that Johann was the first and only Amish person to whom I've ever spoken?

It wasn't just curiosity that made me happy to meet him. It's a truism that we are drawn to those persons who display the qualities we feel are lacking in ourselves. As it happens, the book I'd been reading on this train trip was one of those familiar priest's autobiographies, another on-again, off-again search for a vocation that may not really be there. Here, I thought, was a man who would be a counterpoint to such divagation, a man who would be nothing if not sincere and who literally wore his convictions on his sleeve. I was right; Johann proved completely lacking in irony. We quickly fell into an easy conversation.

Johann was a little more than thirty years old. He wore suspenders and black broadfall trousers, but was not wearing his wide-brimmed hat, which in some Amish communities might be an infraction against the dress code. He and seventeen of his family were traveling from Indiana in order to attend a camp outside Whitefish, Montana. At no point did any of his energetic children—most of them were boys, and they were roughhousing one another around us—distract him from his talk. All of the women in the group, even the youngest, were wearing white bonnets. It puzzled me that he could ride on Amtrak but not own an automobile, and it puzzled me further that his sons were playing with hand-held video games. I would later learn that, although Amish life is crammed with proscriptions, in many areas it is and always has been a ceaseless series of negotiations and accommodations with modernity. Hand-held games run on batteries, and are therefore more allowable than devices that plug into the wall.

But in most ways Johann's life was vastly simpler than my own, or than that of anyone I know. He ran a small farm with the labor of horses, and when he read his German prayer books and his scripture, he did so by daylight or by kerosene lamp. As the train neared the Mississippi River, he wanted to know all about the passing countryside: how high the river flooded, the prosperity of the farms, what sorts of trees grew on the hills. The sight of a bald eagle excited him like a schoolboy.

Our conversation turned to religion. Johann was at ease discussing Amish life and belief—though he often halted to say he could explain things better in German—and forthright about his embrace of the *Ord-*

nung, the elaborate code of behavior that regulates the details of Amish daily life.

He took obvious pride in the demands of worship services among the Amish. "All of our prayers and our church services are in German," he said, "and most of the time that's how we talk to each other, too. Our Sunday services last most of the day. The men and the women sit separate, but everybody knows where to sit.

"Our ministers, they know what the scripture readings are going to be, but they don't know what they are going to preach. They just know that the words of scripture can't be wrong, and that God will lead them to the right words.

"Everybody sings, but we don't have any instruments. We almost always know the words by heart. Our services last about three hours, three and a half hours. That probably seems like a long time to you but it doesn't seem that way to us.

"Then, afterward, we have time to talk about business in the church, and ways that we can help each other, and we eat a meal together. It might be three o'clock in the afternoon before our church is over, that way."

I asked him if it was customary to wear special clothes to church, but he didn't quite answer. He pointed to his black overalls. "People ask us if we think that wearing these clothes will get us into heaven. We absolutely do not. We don't think any such thing, not at all. But I do know that if I wear these clothes, it will keep me out of places where I should not go."

Then I asked him how the Amish selected their clergy.

"We do it by drawing lots," he explained. "When a congregation needs a minister, the bishop comes and interviews every member to ask who they think might be a good candidate.

"Usually there will be three or four men in the community whose names keep coming up. Those three or four men are taken aside in a room, and then the bishop takes the same number of the *Ausbund*—that's the prayer book we all use—and, in one of the books he puts a white slip of paper beside hymn 131, '*Lob Lied*.' It's a song that goes way, way back to Germany, to before the year 1600. No matter what, we sing that hymn at every worship service.

"Then he calls the men back. The men each take a book and they turn to song 131, and whoever draws the white slip, he's the next pastor. Sometimes the men try to mix it up—say , the second man will take the third book—but it doesn't matter. God knows how it will turn out."

I found his earnestness both moving and impressive. After Johann left to tend to something with his wife and children, I sat quietly, looking out the window and reflected about our conversation. The evening sun fell on copses of box elder, on sprouting soybean fields, and sometimes on herons rowing the air slowly from one pond to another along the railroad tracks, indifferent to our passing train. We patronize the Amish, I realized, when we tell ourselves that they are suspicious and fearful of the world. Talking with this young man, it struck me that, rather, his life was organized around an irreducible core of trust. Trust that the *Ordnung* would keep him out of trouble. Trust in simple tools and in work. Trust that his neighbors know best, trust that God knows how things will turn out.

I thought about Johann much of the way home, and thought about how superficial my own life—as well as the life of so many of my family and friends, all busily advancing careers, worrying about money, acquiring new cars and summer homes and CD collections that ran into the thousands—seemed when compared to his embrace of a modest communitarian life on the land. I looked at the lights from newly developed homes built along the river, and I felt sad; the cherished dreams of millions of American homeowners, these little outposts of "acreage," seemed ersatz and painfully lonely. Johann had described a life that quietly said no-thank-you to all this, a life both simpler and more solemn—one lived as if eternity were watching.

Then, just as the train crossed back over the Mississippi about 10:00 P.M., in the moment that we passed over the channel, tumbling below the lock and dam at Hastings, I felt some sort of elemental connection to the river below us. It seemed like the pull of the river current ran through me, too, and ran through all of us. I can't separate it from Johann's lived testimony of trust: I had a glimpse of the certainty that, no matter how many petty acquisitions may accrue on the land or how frivolous our concerns, rivers would still run, and we can be thankful.

In early August, the farm landscape explodes with abundance. The only hint of death near the Amish Cemetery was a tall, barkless cottonwood spar sixty yards away in a soybean field. The trunk has been bleached by the summer and winter suns. Everywhere else, the still-growing cornstalks were green, nearly five feet high, and densely crowded. Across the expanse of the field there were brown growth tassels atop the corn, all at the same level. I found it easy to believe the stories that in the Midwest, there are nights when you can hear the corn grow.

In the daytime, though, the countryside is not necessarily a quiet place; if you pause, you realize how many sounds collect around you. On the August afternoon that I visited the Amish burial ground the wind was everywhere, and a mechanical beat from some machine—a tractor, a well-driller—seemed always in the air. Goldfinches made rising, falling whistles as they skipped their way through the sky. Passing auto tires whined on the blacktop. When a truck shifted gears, the grinding sound was cast across the landscape for miles.

But silence, or the promise of silence, is also near on the prairie; noise and quietude dance around each other like cabbage butterflies above a puddle. Occasionally, all of the noises will stop, and a fragment of the oceanic silence that overwhelmed the first settlers will enfold you for an instant. If you sit quietly beside a trout stream for a long time, you begin to connect to the rhythm of burbling water, yet only grow alert to that rhythm when it's interrupted—if, say, a fish jumps or a stick falls in the water. Something like that happens, when you stand on the prairie and open yourself to its vastness; the speaking wind announces itself only its absence. I stood for a long time trying to catch those moments—certain that somehow, the Amish dead were still there in those moments of noiselessness and wondering whether I might hear them in the fields.

Leathery cornhusks brushed one another. I have read of prayer flags, in Nepal and other Buddhist countries, which are small rectangles or pennants hung along a line outside a temple; the belief is that each flutter of the flag releases a blessing into the world. I wondered if each husk was some version of a prayer, if a field of corn rustling in the wind could fill the air with prayer like sunlight.

There was a presence in the air that was asking me to pray—something in motion like pollen grains, invisible but all around. I sat cross-legged on the scrub grass. The earth gave the sun's heat back. I prayed for the Amish dead by murmuring the old Catholic phrase, over and over: *May perpetual light shine upon them.* A hundred times, tolling it off on my fingers: *May perpetual light shine upon them . . . May perpetual light shine upon them . . . May perpetual light shine upon them.*

I opened my eyes. The wind brushing the cornstalks made the silence nearer, more real. A mourning dove flew off a telephone wire, into the cornstalks. In the soybean field across the gravel road, the wind lifted the leaves erratically. Like something faintly reflected, small flashes of white danced across the deep green.

TRANSLATION

Flat granite stones and sodded-over
ruts from a back-hoe
mark recent graves,
but this land best embraces
those who plowed it first.
Their white marble monuments
stand still, though unevenly,
stained by a century of rain and snow.

I walk among the stones
and guess at German phrases.
Geliebter Mutter. Tochter. Sohn.
The family slots? Long quotes
that must be scripture,
and strange words that often reappear:
Gebet? Errinern? Glaube?
Liebe, love; the one word I know.

HOLY TRINITY CEMETERY, FINGAL, NORTH DAKOTA

(for Mike Morrissey)

It is the circle of distance
that defines the place, and not
the graph of section lines and roads
spaced at right angles
in an old attempt to describe the land.
The horizon surrounds you: a hinge
of earth and sky, into which
bare elements seem to pour,
disappearing into a vanishing point,
out of which the land extrudes
as if flattened by the rollers of a mangle.
A place larger than anyone could imagine.

*

All burial grounds are a mix
of certainty and guesswork.
This one, too:
we are not here given the stories
that attend these Middle European names:
Baumgartner, farming this treeless land,
Seidl, a Czech; a German born in Ungara;
we know only that each needed
to walk away from a mother, a father, a bed,
to cross an ocean, once.

What choice did they have, but to be fearless?

What choice do any of us have,
except to be fearless?

*

A goldfinch pauses on the cemetery fence,
then flies away. Its thin song
is all that answers the wind.

CLOSED FOR THE SEASON

Since 1853, when the Layman family opened a private burial ground at Cedar Avenue and Lake Street in South Minneapolis, there has been a cemetery at the corner of these two arterial streets. I had driven past that intersection many times, and often wondered about the discrepancy between the imposing limestone and wrought-iron fence that surrounds it and the sparsely marked grounds on the other side, but I had never set foot in what is now known as the Old Pioneer Cemetery until I attended a Memorial Day service there in 2002.

That was also the first time I met Susan Hunter Weir, a woman who pursues an ambitious, and thus far, almost solitary, campaign to reclaim both the cemetery's history and its claim on the city's attention. Susan has lived her entire life in South Minneapolis. A great-aunt of hers, who died unnamed at the age of five days in 1901, is buried in the Old Pioneer Cemetery, though Susan did not know that fact until after she began researching in the site. Susan's father was a British citizen, and her mother is of Slovenian descent. In appearance and, it seems, in temperament, she favors her Eastern European side—she has a kind face with dark eyes that often suggest an air of *weltschmerz*. She lives in a neighborhood near the cemetery, an area that is increasingly populated by Somali, Ethiopian, Southeast Asian, and Hispanic immigrants. The neighborhood knows her as a longtime activist who has often served on committees and task forces and helped to plant dozens of community gardens.

Almost no one who ever attended a burial at Old Pioneer Cemetery is still alive today. The recollection of this burial ground's once vigorous role in the community's life erodes further with each year. Recall is not always a passive function; the maintenance of a civic memory requires effort—record-keeping, research, education, storytelling. For the past five years, for reasons that are not completely clear even to herself, Susan Hunter Weir has been doing the work of remembering. She now devotes nearly all of her spare time, including her lunch breaks, to researching interment records and other information about the citizens buried in the Old Pioneer, a project that her family calls "Susan's peculiar passion." Thus far she has compiled 3,000 typescript pages of documentation, and she has another forty-five years' worth of records left to examine.

For six decades, the burial ground that she has adopted was known as the Layman Cemetery, or simply as the Minneapolis Cemetery, and until the cemetery association stopped selling gravesites in 1919 because of overcrowding, the grounds received the remains of approximately 25,000 early citizens of Minneapolis. At least 15,000 of these graves were never marked.

Around 1920, descendants of the founding family arranged to have the remains of about 7,000 persons exhumed and reinterred elsewhere in anticipation of either a baseball park or a large streetcar barn. Neither the ballpark nor the barns were built. After the prospect of real estate development vanished, the Layman family lost any prospect of financial return from the site, and their interest in the cemetery site faded. In 1927, the city of Minneapolis purchased the cemetery from the family and, mindful of its long history, renamed it the Old Pioneer Cemetery. The city's Parks Board has been responsible for the place ever since. The WPA writers' project inventoried the cemetery in 1939 and recorded 2,500 monuments. More than 500 of those monuments have subsequently been lost to vandalism and inattention.

The Parks Board keeps the cemetery open to the public from April 15 to October 15. The rest of the year it is closed for the season, though a metal sign on the Cedar Avenue gates provides a number to call to arrange a visit. Few such visits are ever scheduled. Trees and shrubbery of uneven sizes and species are scattered throughout the grounds, which cover twenty-seven acres. Five tall poplars in the center of the grounds have died for some reason, but their dead trunks have not been removed. The gravestones vary in design but all are modest. In some ways, the Old Pioneer is a sort of micro-Appalachia, a worn-down place that survives by grudging government support.

A strong military cast shaped the Memorial Day observance at which I met Susan; with a few changes, it mirrored similar ceremonies I had attended as a child. The Seward Concert Band, a community orchestra from an adjoining neighborhood, performed "America the Beautiful," "Battle Hymn of the Republic," and Sousa marches. As the band struck up a medley of the service hymns, the veterans of each service rose for their song. A Navy veteran who looked to be well over eighty struggled to rise for "Anchors Aweigh," then cried as he removed his VFW cap. The featured speaker was a Colonel Mike Mihelich, an Air Force recruiter. The program included a reading of the Gettysburg Address declaimed by Nimo Afyare, a Somali tenth-grade high school student; later, she also read "General Logan's Order #11," the 1867 proclamation setting aside this day in May in perpetuity. I happened to be seated next to an African man in a badly fitting white sport coat, whom I assumed was her father. He beamed with pride.

Susan was introduced as a local historian, and she spoke only a few minutes, confining her remarks to a few stories that she had come across in the course of researching the cemetery. Among these were the grave of an African-American man named Woodford Anderson, who fought in one of the "colored" regiments in the Civil War, for whom she is trying to replace the crumbling headstone. All veterans are entitled to such a marker (though Susan also wishes to preserve the historic stone). She told of an iron cross around which a tree trunk had grown. It had marked the grave of a six-month-old boy named John Herman Graeni, who died in 1884. She had found a metalsmith in the University of Minnesota art department to recast the cross, and was having it reerected.

The burial about which she spoke most extensively was that of John Effert, a Russian immigrant who died at age twenty-six in a railway accident, and whose 1911 gravestone bears a Socialist Worker's Party insignia with clasped hands over the globe and the collectivist legend "Workers of the World Unite." She would later tell me that when the ceremony was over, the single most commended portion of her talk was her evocation of the forgotten radical. Her claiming of a place for the outsider and the obscure seemed almost daring in a setting calculated to evoke triumphalism. This was only a half-year or so after the September 11 attacks.

The gathering dispersed after a brief wreath-laying ceremony and a twenty-one-gun salute. As the crowd was breaking up, I fell in with a group of a half-dozen other people walking with Susan, who had started an impromptu tour. She was leading them to John Effert's grave in the northwest corner of the grounds.

The old socialist's burial site is well placed, for a victim of industrial violence: railroad tracks run along that edge of the cemetery, and his grave overlooks a municipal solid waste transfer station and the Smith Iron Foundry. His monument is a modest dark granite stone, about twenty inches tall. The socialist insignia is carved less deeply than his name, leading Susan to speculate whether it was added later.

Someone asked Susan who was the most famous person buried there.

She answered, "This has always been the poor people's cemetery. None of the early mayors or founding families are here. Most of the big names are almost all down at Lakewood Cemetery." Lakewood is a large and well looked-after burial ground about a mile south of downtown Minneapolis.

"But to answer your question, the most famous person is undoubtedly Harry Hayward. He was a prominent man-about-town who took out a life insurance policy of $10,000 on his mistress. He hired a man named Klaus Blix to take her on a carriage ride around Lake Calhoun, and murder her while he was at the opera. For Minneapolis in the 1890s, it was as sensational as the O. J. Simpson trial. Even after he was convicted, he had a following. There were often bouquets of roses left at Harry's grave. He has a big monument over in that corner of the cemetery." She pointed toward Lake Street.

I needed to leave to attend a family picnic, but before I excused myself I told Susan how much I appreciated her efforts. She invited me to drop in on her at the cemetery office some weekend. "I'll be there going through the files," she said. "For the last four summers, I've only missed two or three weekends. Before you go I want you to take a look at the garage." We walked to a small wooden building just north of the cemetery office.

"I don't know when this was built," she said, "sometime around 1970, I think. It doesn't matter. Take a look at the foundation." About half of the blocks in the foundation bore numbers, but they were not aligned in any order. They were tossed together like a wall built with a child's set of blocks.

"Those are the old section markers from the cemetery," she explained. "Last year, I spent a huge amount of time figuring out the numbering system from the big plat book kept in the office. I ended up redrawing and numbering the cemetery map, because somewhere along the line, somebody decided that it wasn't important to be able to find the graves anymore. Maybe years had gone by and nobody had asked. They were probably hard to mow around, too—so they just tore them out and built a garage with them instead."

It was not until a Saturday morning in September that I got around to dropping in on Susan. I parked my car on Twenty-First Avenue, at the eastern end of the cemetery. Unlike Memorial Day, on this day only the entrance at the western end was open, and I needed to walk several blocks to get to the gates. Lake Street was busy. At the corner of Lake and Cedar, a group of East African women in saffron-and-sage-colored *jallabib* were waiting for the bus, and I wondered whether it seemed odd to them to wait in front of a place consecrated to someone else's memories. Cars sped by and a song by Santana played at Señor G's tavern. The graying stones behind the fence conveyed a quality of stillness, all the same.

The place seemed more tired than it had when I first saw it. Many of the monuments were in disrepair. Some have been fitted back together with tar and a rubbery sort of glue, and others have been left in disconnected pieces. The city does a good job of picking up litter; the only trash I saw was a golf ball that had been clipped by a lawnmower blade. When I picked it up from the base of a headstone, the once tightly wound core fell out raggedly.

The cemetery office is a rectangular fieldstone building constructed in 1873. Besides housing cemetery records, the Park Board uses the building to store cleaning supplies, shovels, rakes, and miscellaneous items including—inexplicably—an upright piano. The office has the look and feel of a rarely visited workplace, like a janitor's office or the cabin of a tugboat. Unmarked boxes are stacked on top of one another, electric fans sit atop file cabinets, and the walls are painted an institutional green. A calendar from a cleaning supply company hangs on a wall. An electric clock that is six hours behind and a framed aerial photograph of the cemetery hang on another wall. A bedraggled clutter of tables and chairs and a mismatched assortment of file cabinets and safes fill the rest of the room.

Susan remembered me and introduced me to Denny Berquist, the cemetery caretaker. He is a husky, broad-faced man from Chicago (he looks a little like Anthony Quinn) who speaks in a booming voice. When I walked in, Denny was telling Susan about the dead starlings and crows on the grounds, which he feared might mean the West Nile Virus had arrived in Minnesota. Susan sat at a desk cluttered with papers, coffee cups, and two yellow hardhats. Four steel file trays, each containing hundreds of index cards, were in front of her.

I sat down on a pea-green upholstered chair. She helped Denny log on to his e-mail—it was clear that this was a familiar ritual for her—and while he pored over his accumulated messages, she turned to me.

"John Effert is the one who first got me interested in the cemetery," she said. "I don't remember why it was, but for some reason my husband and I came here, and met Denny. Denny told us about some of the more unusual monuments, and he mentioned a labor organizer who had died in an accident who had a Socialist insignia on his headstone. As soon as I heard that, I thought to myself, 'This is a story I'd like to know more about.' Fool that I was, I thought that if somebody had been killed in a railroad accident the papers would all cover the story.

"Then, when I went to the microfilm at the Hennepin County History center, there was nothing in any of the papers. Nothing. Zilch. But I just kept thinking I could find out something about him. I started to check the city directories, and then I started to read all the radical papers on microfilm. What I wanted to know was not so much about how he died, but 'Who cared about this man while he was alive?'

"I even went so far as to find out the name of the monument company for his headstone from the cemetery records—it cost $3.50—and called up that company. I spent three months trying to find out about John Effert, and then I got to a point when I realized I had done everything that could be done. There was just no more available to me at the time. This was all pre-internet, or, at least, before the Ellis Island records were online. Then, when the Ellis Island lists became available, I typed his name in and, boom! there he was. He was five feet, six inches tall, blond and blue eyed, and had arrived alone in New York City in 1906. I just looked at the screen and wept because I had found him.

"It dawned on me that his was one of a huge number of stories that just never got reported. Immigrant workers were dying all the time.

"One thing led to another, and I got connected to Dawn Wangen, a historian who is trying to compile a computerized guide to the Phillips neighborhood in 1909. She wants to set it up so that there's a map, and when you click on any house you can call up the whole history of that house and the people who lived there. It's going to be really impressive. I turn over what I find to Dawn and she puts it on the computer. I'm not a technical person at all. But I was interested in the connections between the Phillips neighborhood and this cemetery.

"Then after a while, I started to feel differently about the project. There's just an incredible amount on information in these records. You can link practically anybody buried here to families still in the city. But I don't want just a database or a genealogy; what I want is . . . I guess what I want is the city that they lived in."

She placed her hand, palm-down, on one of the file drawers. "It's important to me to know that there are the real bones of dead people in this place," she said.

"As I got more and more into this, something else happened, and that was that I somehow started to feel responsible for the people buried here and for their stories. You probably read the article about Anna Clark in the paper. When her family came to me and asked if I would help with a memorial service. It was one of the most moving experiences of my life."

Anna L. Clark was a fifty-four-year-old widow who had shot herself in 1909. Life had been brutal for her; eight of her sixteen children had died in infancy. She spent her last nickel to take a streetcar to this cemetery, where, standing on the unmarked grave of her husband who'd died four years before, she put a revolver to her temple. Her suicide note said, "Bury me beside papa, if you think I am worthy of it." She was buried next to him, but the grave remained unmarked for ninety-two years until a descendant learned of the story and arranged to have a stone monument erected.

"Anna was unusual because she used a gun. We have at least a hundred suicides in here, and almost all of them either hung themselves or drank carbolic acid, which was a horrible way to die."

Carbolic acid, she added, was a common rat poison. "The brand name was 'Rough on Rats.' When people drank it, the acid ate through the stomach and they suffered agony until they died of internal bleeding. But it was how poor people killed themselves. Right after the Civil War, there were six or eight veterans who shot themselves. I discovered later that a lot of them had been given their army rifles as part of their discharge.

"There are at least 164 Civil War veterans buried here," she continued, "though I think the actual number is probably much higher than that.

Every one of them is entitled to a government-issued marker. I know we have three veterans from the War of 1812 and I think it's twenty-one from the Spanish-American War. The cemetery stopped being an active cemetery during the First World War so, as far as I know, we only have one veteran from that war."

"We got a few Johnnie Rebs, too," said Denny, using a term I had not heard in decades. He pointed to the aerial photograph. "One of them's buried over in that corner."

When was that picture taken?" I asked.

"I think about 1930," Denny said instantly. "One of those black cars is a 1929 Oldsmobile and it looks new."

Susan said, "I'm sure that an awful lot of those Civil War vets had post-traumatic stress syndrome, just like a lot of men who came back from Vietnam.

"Sometimes you can get another sort of problem when you start looking into these stories—knowing how much you should expose. Last year at the Memorial Day service we mentioned Benjamin Rackliff, who was a decorated veteran of the Civil War and also a prisoner at the Andersonville camp. But I also know that in 1884 he beat and kicked his wife to death. What do you do with that sort of information? I guess you just need to be compassionate when you can, and tell yourself that it's all part of history now."

"The University of Minnesota used to bury their experiments here," Denny said. "Did you know that?"

"I did," said Susan. "They weren't exactly experiments, though. In those days the cadavers of a lot of indigent people ended up being used for teaching purposes at the medical school, and they all ended up being buried here. None of the graves were marked, of course.

"There were a lot of violent deaths, but, of course, most of the time what you find are families who got wiped out when there was an outbreak of disease. The violent ones can be pretty grisly. We have one family here called Libby. Gustave Libby was a German immigrant. He had three sons. One committed suicide with carbolic acid when he was twenty-three. Another one, Henry, put his head on a railroad track and was decapitated when he was twenty-eight. And the third one was a terrible alcoholic and drank himself to death."

Denny got up from his chair. "That's a cheerful story," he said. He walked to the back room and began organizing a pile of rakes and other tools that had fallen to the floor.

Susan smiled. "The fact is, I'm not morbid at all." she said. "When people tease me about being obsessed with dead people, I tell them, 'No, I have an agreement with the dead: they stay on their side and I stay on mine.' Do the dead talk to me? Sure—but they do it by way of these burial records, or in all the things I've learned from the newspapers and other accounts."

Susan paused. She picked up one of the hardhats on the desk, and stared at it as if it were an archaeological discovery. In a minute she said, "There is one thing that's changed about me since I starting looking into this place. I used to tell my husband I wanted to be cremated. Not any more. Now I want a burial. I'm not sure why that is."

I made a connection, in my mind, between what Susan had said and a line in a poem by Lisa Coffman: *"flesh maps what we lose."* If we thought of a place like the Old Pioneer Cemetery as being a library of 18,000 such maps—as if each of the bodies buried here was, in some mysterious way, a sort of memoir writing, another contribution to the world's store of lessons learned—then interment seems a fitting end. An unwritten history is not necessarily a forgotten history; indeed, if we conceive of our physical remains as having charted a life, there might not be as much unwritten history as we think.

Susan continued to talk. Her knowledge of the city was encyclopedic, and as she spoke it became clear that her work amounted to more than a grassroots revision of the city's past. Revising the past, letting the world know that the received written history of Minneapolis—a chronicle of ambitious and entrepreneurial New Englanders, blue-eyed Yankee boys who fought in the Civil War, and, later, hardworking Scandinavians— was only a partial account, was a first step in her project. At a deeper level, though, Susan's project was positing an epistemology of history itself, a way of apprehending the world as an unending web of stories. I told her one of my own: how, in a single week, my great-grandparents had lost four children to diphtheria.

"One of the things that bothers me," Susan said, "is when we say today, 'Oh, life was hard back then, people were more used to suffering.' There was a lot more death nearby, back then, but I don't think they ever got used to it. I read the letters that the wife of a Swedish immigrant wrote, or, rather, had his wife wrote for him, after his sixteen-year-old daughter died. The poor man was just devastated. Her name was Ruth Christine Samuelson. I don't know the father's name; in the letter, he is just 'papa.'"

She paused and shuffled through some papers in a manila folder.

"I can't find it now," she said "but I wanted to show you the funeral card from a nine-year old-boy buried here. He has a great name: Toussaint L'Overture Gray. Named after the Haitian hero. He died of heart disease when he was nine.

"Actually, I found out a lot about that family: his father, Ralph Gray, was a barber at the Northwestern Hotel downtown, and he grew prize-winning radishes. The newspapers would have stories about how Ralph Gray showed off his giant radishes every summer.

"Anyway, the funeral card was very sentimental, but you know how sometimes a simple phrase will just capture you? There was one line in it that touched me: the phrase, 'Gone to Glory Before Us.' I find that very moving. If I ever get around to putting this information into a book, I think that will be the title: "Gone to Glory Before Us.""

It was close to noon. I needed to get home, and so thanked Susan and Denny for their time. Susan walked out with me. It was still cool, one of those cloudy early autumn days that signaled a change in the rhythm of the year.

Susan remarked, "We've gotten the cemetery designated as a national Arbor Day site, by the way. Next May, the city will plant a 150 trees of all varieties here. It wasn't easy to persuade the city. You know bureaucrats— they were deathly afraid that we'd plant trees on an unmarked grave, and the relatives would sue. Of course, if they were unmarked, the relatives would not know in the first place."

I asked if she knew how many of the unmarked graves were those of children.

"At least half," she said. "That includes the first person buried here, a Baptist minister's son named Carlton K. Cressey who died of consumption when he was ten months old. Remember, not many poor parents could afford headstones. If you see one of those fancy stones with a little lamb on it, you can bet that the parents were well-off."

I noticed that the top branches of a large cedar tree near the office appeared to have been broken; it had probably been damaged in a windstorm, and should have been trimmed or taken down years ago.

Aesthetically, the Old Pioneer grounds struck me as pathetically inadequate to express the humanity of the place. It was hard not to think that Susan's efforts to rescue the dead from anonymity—not to mention the ten thousand pinpricks of recollection that this cemetery evoked in families both distant and near—deserved a more graceful tribute. In *The City in History*, Lewis Mumford proposes that the first cities sprang up when early peoples wished to remain near the burial places of their ancestors. Looking at the jumble of new businesses that surrounded this place—a Maaco Muffler Repair, a boarded-up Jiffy gas station, the Dur Dur Ethiopian grocery—it was hard to sense that connection. The cars on Lake Street moved east and west in the fitful stream of city traffic. In front of the Salvation Army store across the street, three Hispanic men peered under the hood of a car. Yet, these grounds kept an unbroken link to the city's earliest days. The fact that this remained a set-aside place, unaltered in its purpose since the first burial in 1853, and the plain reality that flesh and bone were buried here and were looked after was sufficient, was itself an honor. An army of gardeners and arborists could do no better.

We walked toward Cedar Avenue. Except for a group of three teenaged girls smoking just inside the gates, no one else was on the grounds.

Susan asked, "Did I tell you about the eight incubator babies from Wonderland?" I must have looked perplexed, because she explained herself immediately. "Wonderland was an amusement park on Thirty-First and Lake. This sounds incredible, but one of the ways that the earliest research on incubators was funded was by showing the premature babies in sideshows. A German doctor named Martin Couney was a pioneer in the field. He tried out some of his earliest devices right down the street at Wonderland. "

"Eight of the Wonderland babies are buried here. You have to remember, even though it sounds terrible, it was a good thing to do—sort of like being an organ donor today. Parents knew that those tiny babies were doomed, so they let them be shown to raise money for research.

"You find some awful things, though. Maybe the worst is Hans Offedal. In 1908, he opened a hospital for orphans at 3341 Nicollet. Offedal claimed to be a doctor, but when he turns up in the city directories twenty years later they list him as a roofing contractor. One day in 1909 he turned off the utilities and moved away, and left five abandoned children behind, who would have died if the authorities hadn't rescued them. During the year he was pretending to be a doctor, twenty-three orphans died in his 'hospital.' They're all buried here, too."

I said, "That's such a sad story."

"Oh," Susan said, "there's just no end to the sadness, once you start looking." Then she shook my hand, and went back to the office to do more research.

BETWEEN SEASONS

It is the last warm Sunday in October.
Days like this are a wasting asset.
We know the forecast.

Nearby, headstones lean
against the wrought, geographic trunks
of old junipers.

Back in August, someone mowed;
now goldenrod is belt-high,
aspens are nearly bare. In a month

no more than two leaves will remain
at the trees' terminal bud,
hanging on into thin winter.

On the branches, leaf scars
are being born as leaves fall,
a dozen or more a minute.

They drop in quiet witness
on this last warm Sunday.
One by one, breaking

away from their nodes
with small cracking sounds,
like freezing rain hitting a window.

SHIELDSVILLE CHURCHYARD, NOVEMBER

Even the daylight hours are cooler now.
The start of deer season: orange-vested hunters

enter or come out of the nearly bare woods.
In the cemetery, the well-tended grass,

is still green. But in the pasture next to it,
powdery goldenrod fronds sag on dry stalks.

Sparrows flit between them and the box-elders.
One granite headstone bearing the name Reilly

is dotted with hundreds of Asian beetles.
They do not move. Perhaps they're dead already.

From a woodlot a mile in the distance,
a rifle shot punctuates the chilling world.

IN THE DRIFTLESS AREA

I cannot recall now who first suggested that I visit Old Frontenac Cemetery, but if I could, I would thank that person. I like for places to have a pedigree; to be told, when going on a trip, about some scenic backroad that I will later come to claim as my own, or to plan picnics and go hiking where friends have recommended. As friends and colleagues have come to know that I have an interest in graveyards, I have often been steered toward one or another such site, in the same way that gardeners might hand on root bundles and cuttings to one another's perennial bed.

I've traveled the stretch of Highway 61 that runs along the southeastern border of Minnesota on many trips in the past, visiting college friends in Winona or, before that, with my dad and brother on their outdoorsman trips. Then, three years ago, my son became a college student in southern Wisconsin. In the course of comings and goings to his school I quickly learned what little taste I have for the busy hundred miles of Interstate Highway 94 that run east of the Twin Cities. A more pleasant alternate route is to drive down the western side of the Mississippi River as far south as LaCrosse, Wisconsin, and then pick up Interstate 90. I've taken this circuit a dozen times in the past three years. The lighter traffic and the scenery more than compensate for the extra hour the route requires.

This itinerary passes through what geologists call "the driftless area" of the upper Mississippi valley, a region left untouched by the last glaciers. When the rest of Minnesota lay under a relentless sheet of ice, this area was spared, and today when you drive along Highway 61 and catch glimpses of streams in riven valleys bubbling toward the Mississippi, or of cattle grazing on hillsides below rounded bluff-tops, the agreeable topography that you are passing is that way in part because of a geological amnesty 12,000 to 18,000 years ago.

I had always assumed that Frontenac was a mere whistlestop between Red Wing and Lake City. I dabble at bird-watching, and have often meant to visit the state park there, where trails along the bluffs are known to be a fine place to spot both warblers and migrating birds of prey every spring and fall. When I drove through in mid-October, a screech owl was roosting in a front-yard tree. By the time I realized what I had seen, I was a mile down the road. But I had never stopped in Frontenac until last year, when, on the Sunday after Thanksgiving, I made another excursion (my third since August) to deliver my son to the Greyhound station in LaCrosse where he could catch a bus the rest of the way back to school.

My son's bus was to leave at 12:05. We got to the station with only a few minutes to spare and said our good-byes as he lined up to board. I crossed the river back into Minnesota—the bridge on Highway 14 towers above the Mississippi, and its metal grid deck produces strange, unsettling tugs on your steering wheel—and as I drove through French Island and the river bottoms, I made up my mind that I would not hurry back home. Instead, I made a plan to stop for lunch, have a cup of coffee in Winona, buy a peck of Regent apples at one of the orchards near Lake Pepin, and to take another break in Frontenac and finally visit the cemetery that had been recommended to me. I wondered if perhaps it held very old graves dating back to the eighteenth century when French-Canadian fur traders had made Frontenac a trapping outpost.

The date was November 25. A string of unprecedented temperatures in the sixties had lasted right up until the week of Thanksgiving, but the fantasy that such weather might continue had blown away in the night. As I filled my car at an Amoco station in LaCrescent, on the Minnesota side, I watched a styrofoam cup rattle down the middle of the road, ahead of the wind, and it made me think of January blizzards. I told the clerk that it looked like winter was going to come after all, and she said, yes it did—but that it had been nice and warm yesterday.

There was no question that the weather was about to turn. Looking up the river, I thought snow might already be falling in some of the coulees, and along the highway, in the steely backwaters that dotted the marshes, there were waves as dark and mutinous as those on Gabriel Conroy's Shannon.

But no snow fell as I drove toward home. I stopped at a Subway Sandwich shop, and in Winona, drank two cups of coffee at a café called The Blue Heron, near the state university. Only three other people were there, bookish young women deep in their studies. All the way north, the river on my right rolled majestic and empty, though below Wabasha I marveled at an enormous tow of sixteen barges, being steered willfully downstream. The late season hillsides were leafless. On some, the tilted white trunks of birch trees stood out like the feathering of frost on a windowpane. Most of the landscape could have been drawn solely with the colors a child would choose last from a box of crayons—brown, gray, and burnt sienna—except for showers of yellow leaves that were weeping willows, and the still-green lawns of farmyards. After driving past three roadside orchards, the place in Lake City where I had intended to stop for apples turned out to be closed for the season.

Traffic was heavier than usual. The other drivers all seemed pressured to get somewhere fast. I cruised a few miles above the speed limit but even along the twisting, two-lane sections, cars passed me. I reached Frontenac at three o'clock, where I stopped at another Amoco station, under an enormous red-and-blue sign. I parked in front of a locked case of propane tanks, left my car running, and asked for directions to the cemetery from a young man of about fifteen who needed a shave, or more likely, who needed to have someone tell him he needed a shave.

He gave his directions entirely in landmarks: "The graveyard in Old Frontenac? Go down this road, around the oil tanks. Turn right at the highway, and go about a mile until you see a pond. Turn right again, and when you get to the ballfield, go left."

I found the cemetery easily, surprised that it was in the midst of the village of Old Frontenac, a string of small but comfortable older homes. In one, an inverted duck boat lay in the middle of the front yard; in another yard, a homeowner was stringing Christmas lights. Two brick pillars stood at the entrance to the cemetery. A nearby sign read "Old Frontenac Cemetery. Gate Closes at 8:30 P.M." I saw no gate.

Except for an acre or so of newer plots to the right of the pillars, Old Frontenac Cemetery sits entirely on a narrow strip of land atop a ridge. A rutted, one-lane road runs along the crown of the ridge, with the burial sites on either side of the road, most of them at a slight slope. I wondered if some were buried with their feet higher than their heads—surely an irrelevant consideration, but I wondered nonetheless.

The cemetery is shaped a little like a bobby pin; the dirt road at its center turns subtly at several places, and loops around at the far end. This makes it an intimate place. Wherever you stand, the cemetery appears smaller than its actual extent. The dense growth of surrounding trees had lost every hint of foliage, but the space felt enclosed. The grounds showed obvious care in landscaping and maintenance, and, judging by the number of flags denoting where a veteran lie, and by a number of bouquets left on gravesites, were still visited. On a grave marked by a stone that read "Winnie," a basket of cloth tulips sat on the cold earth. Winnie had died in 1896. I stopped next to a large grove of junipers, away from the unexpectedly sharp wind, and watched juncoes flash their white tail feathers as they flitted in and out of the brush.

Enclosed plots surrounded by iron fences lined the road every hundred yards or so. The care given the grounds impressed me: it was litter-free and fully raked. Encroaching brush had been cut back and lay in piles off to the side. I kept walking, in spite of the cold. By the time I reached the most imposing monuments at the end of the road—the tombs of the Garrard family, who, I would later learn, were the first family of this village during its years as a nineteenth-century resort community spoken of as the "Newport of the Northwest"—I was shivering. My nose was running, but, recalling stories about how deer hunters were shot when their handkerchief was mistaken for the flash of a deer's tail, I wiped it on my jacket sleeve.

At the far end of the graveyard, I spotted the only piece of trash I had seen since arriving—a plastic Mountain Dew bottle in the woods. It offended me; I carried it back to my car to throw away later, and discarded it at the first trash barrel I saw. I left Old Frontenac Cemetery to the coming snow, certain that I would return.

Winter came. For Minnesota, it was a gentle season, which rarely dipped below zero, but all the same it was winter—a span of dark, claustrophobic months that lies at the heart of life in a Northern climate.

I passed through Frontenac again while bringing my son home for the Christmas holidays. On the trip I swung by the cemetery but did not stop. I jotted down the phone numbers of the cemetery association posted near its entrance, whom I hoped to call sometime in the spring. During the winter I consulted Minnesota history books and learned the broad outlines of the region's history. I had been fanciful in thinking it went back to French fur-trading days, though the first Christian chapel in Minnesota had been built here by the French, in 1727. Old Frontenac had been settled in the late 1830s by a Dutch immigrant named Westervelt—that was a name I recalled seeing in the graveyard—and had been developed into a fashionable resort in the years following the Civil War, visited by President U.S. Grant and the Beecher family of clergymen. The entire village is on the National Register of Historic Places.

The late end of winter can be ugly and ragged in this part of the world. Snowbanks survive in jagged heaps, and the first thaws uncover dirty leaves and matted grass tamped flat by the snows, old paper, and dog droppings charred by winter. But a certain kind of buoyancy arrives with these melting days all the same. On March 29, Good Friday, it was clear that the tilt toward spring was irreversible. Weather forecasts predicted that it might approach sixty degrees. At my neighborhood coffee shop that morning it struck me that it would be a good day to revisit Old Frontenac Cemetery. An acquaintance there, Ken Johnson, said he'd like to ride along, and by 9:15 I had called one of the numbers I'd taken down the previous December and arranged to meet Peter Webster, the treasurer of the cemetery association, at the cemetery entrance at 11:00 A.M.

It's easy to grow impatient for spring in Minnesota; some of the time as Ken and I drove through Pine Bend, Hastings, and Red Wing en route to Frontenac, we rode with the windows down. In Hastings we noticed a teenaged boy walking with his shirt off. It was only about fifty-five degrees. His skin was as pale as a fish's belly. As we passed the entrance to the state park, I noticed the park's mailbox had been clipped by a snowplow, crimped like a folded-over boot. Sparrow hawks had begun their migration. They perched on telephone wires, peering over the warming fields for the first stirrings of gophers and mice, and it seemed as if the very hillsides and bluffs along the Mississippi welcomed the light, absorbed it like arthritic retirees who've just arrived in Scottsdale.

We got there precisely at 11:00. I don't know what I had expected my cemetery guide to be like—maybe some ardent local historian, or a rustic type with a noble obsession for honoring the dead—but in fact, Peter Webster was a handsome, tall man of about seventy, a retired businessman who in his work life had been a banker in Lake City. He was the sort of man who gave the impression of having always been comfortable being in charge, and that he enjoyed looking after details and solving problems. Fifteen years ago he took up the position of treasurer for the cemetery association. He had brought along a plat map of the cemetery, hand-drawn in 1937 and big as a tablecloth; we unrolled it and held it flat between us. I admired the Spencerian script of the text.

"The cemetery first started with a gift from General Israel Garrard," he explained. "You'll see his house when you go into town. He was a very prominent Civil War general, from Cincinnati originally. The family gave a lot of property to the park and the town, and it has to be used for the purposes for which they gave it. If it's not, it will revert back to the family. There are still descendants, in Minneapolis and in Sedona, Arizona.

"It's still a working cemetery and as you can see there are still lots of burial plots that haven't been sold. We sell them for $350, and what you get is a perpetual care agreement; you don't get a cemetery deed. We'd like to clear out some of the brush and trees and open even more space."

Ken remarked that $350 was less than half of what he pays for rent each month in St. Paul.

I told Mr. Webster I admired the order and tidiness of the site, particularly as in country graveyards I had gotten used to seeing places that have been neglected. The compliment pleased him. "We pay a lawn service that comes out from Red Wing to look after it twice a month and they do a good job," he said. "And when I joined the association, I made sure to go to the sheriff's office in Lake City so that offenders can be sentenced to service by helping here. They rake it every fall. I used to have the inmates from the boys' reform school in Red Wing work at it, but they didn't do a good job."

We turned to walk into the older burial grounds. I asked which was the oldest grave here. "To be honest, I don't know. I'm not really that much of a cemetery historian, and if you want local history I'll have to direct you to my brother, Bill Webster, or to somebody else. A lot of the older headstones are in German," he said. "We've had two vandalism incidents in the past ten years, and some of them have broken into six pieces. We don't have as many records as you might think about the early years, but we do have mortuary records for every burial, going back to the 1930s."

It was true that more stones lay in piles than I recalled from my previous visit. An 1871 stone rested against the trunk of a tall Scotch pine. It took some time to discern the name Nicolaus Poppe, and the dates of his birth and death. The stone had broken off from the words below. Yet, even when stones were fractured, it also was clear that the caretakers tried to keep the fragments together. I have seen too many cemeteries where old headstones have been left to scatter like dropped flowerpots. It struck me as a laudable act to try to keep these pieces together, to try to honor the fact that these stones had once borne meaning, and that being broken hadn't caused the meaning to vanish. And many of the older headstones were remarkably well preserved. We stopped to look at one for a J. Heinrich Schmid, who died in 1869. A recent wooden cross had been placed in front of it, and on the wood, letters or numbers had been written with a felt-tip marker. Those markings had faded beyond legibility, while the stone could be read as clearly as a newspaper.

"There's so many trees that we don't get much sun in here," Mr. Webster observed. "It's hard to get grass to grow." Much of the ground cover was moss, which even now, after lying under snow all winter, retained its color—a green that at places broke into an unexpected vividness. He pointed out a trail of deer tracks sunk deep into the moss.

I stopped to admire a tall monument that said HAKENSON, a large tapered column on a block of stone crowned by a cross. Looking up, beyond the cross, I saw a seagull circling above, its white breast glinting in the sun and blue sky. A crow flew past below it in a straight line.

"This base here," Mr. Webster said, "is Frontenac Sandstone. If you go into the state park you can see the old quarry where they used to cut rock. It was sent all over the country, New York and Washington and everywhere else. But this stone here only traveled about a mile." Burrings and saw marks were still clear on the cream-colored stone. For all I knew, the quarry man who cut it may be buried here himself. I noticed that the nearby headstones had variant spellings, Hakanson and Hainkenson. The phrase "carved in stone" may define permanence, but record of the stones shows just how fluid names and language have always been.

We had reached the end of the cemetery road and the Garrard family plot. These are heavy, above-ground crypts, made from the regional sandstone. General Israel Garrard had died in 1901, in the same week that Teddy Roosevelt became president. His formidable grave was completely of a piece with that era, self-confident to the point of being imperial. A bronze star for the GAR, the Grand Army of the Republic, stood at the foot of his grave. Even in death he commanded deference. The road loops around the tombs, which are cordoned off with heavy chains draped between concrete stanchions. "That's the general, there, and this is his brother," Mr. Webster said as he pointed at the slabs. "And his children. This little stone over here that says M.D. is for Marie Dressler, who was a famous actress in her day. It used to be over there"—he waved at the brush beyond the road—"but we had it moved."

"So she's not buried here?" Ken asked.

"No," he said, "But she was great friends with the general and often visited him."

I said that the term for a funereal marker removed from the actual remains is a cenotaph.

"Is that so?" said Mr. Webster. He scratched at some lichen growing on the flat tops of the tombs.

"We've talked about having these slabs sandblasted, and somebody in the association said you can get high-pressure water nozzles now that are just as good as sandblasting. But we don't have any water on the grounds." I suggested that some preservationists made a case for not interfering with the process of decay, and instead of trying to restore older sites, try to see them stabilized as a ruin.

Mr. Webster dismissed the idea. He pointed to the Webster plot across the lane. "My brother and I had our grandparents' stone sandblasted a few years ago and it turned out nice and clean," he said. He added as a matter of interest, "That gray stone in the back—that's me and my wife."

We began walking toward our cars. Ken and I opened a gate and entered a small square family plot, marked off by a rusted iron fence. There are a half dozen or so such plots along the road. Some of these fences lean from subsidence, but most stand as firm as when they were first set. Ken tolled off the letters of a name as he rubbed his hand over the letters at the base of a headstone: "S-c-h-e-n-n-o-c-h."

"Schennoch," Mr. Webster said. "That's an old name around here. I think I just saw a Schennoch in the Lake City paper, on the volunteer fire department."

I asked Mr. Webster if he knew of any burials outside the boundaries of the cemetery or any unmarked graves. "No," he said, "not exactly. But we just passed one unusual thing. Some girls spread the ashes of a young fellow who died of AIDS back in the woods, and put a plaque on a tree. I can show you, if you like."

Ken and I said we would like to see it, and so we backtracked to the end of the road, about a hundred feet from the Garrard plot. A metal sign—a small, brass-plated marker of the sort sold in hardware stores—was nailed to an elm, down a muddy slope at the edge of the surrounding woods. We picked our way down. In engraved script it read, "In Memory of Christopher Paul B____ 1959–1994. The Lake City Girls." The ashes, of course, had long vanished.

It was hard to know how to respond to this impromptu memorial. The gesture struck me as slight and somehow unearned—as if, whoever these people were, they had only borrowed a sense of place at the fringe of this carefully groomed burial ground. I asked Mr. Webster if he knew anything more about Christopher B____ or the women who took it on themselves to memorialize him. He did not.

As we walked toward the road, Ken told a story of how, the previous summer, he had helped to scatter the ashes of a friend who'd died of cancer. The friend had asked that they be sprinkled from a campsite at Gooseberry Falls into the waters of Lake Superior.

"He left very clear directions about how he wanted it done," Ken said. "Most of us at the scattering had camped there with him. It was a special place for him."

But—and I didn't know how to say it, at the time, and made no comment—I realized that what Ken had just said had something to do with what troubled me about the scattering of the young man's ashes. I had no doubt that Christopher B____ and the Lake City Girls, whoever they were (and they were no more unknown to me than any of the names I passed) loved this locality. They may well have walked together down this cemetery lane, just as Ken and I were doing at this moment, and their shared time together made it a special place for them.

But to Peter Webster and the cemetery association, it was a special place already. Spaces such as this cemetery do not, in the end, derive their meaning from the perceptions and emotional attachments of the deceased or those who are left behind; to suggest that they do is to introduce a note of self-importance that undermines the numinous, even sacramental quality of place itself. Remembrance needs to lead us away from ourselves and into connectedness and awe before all that is greater than ourselves—not to celebrate the snowflake, but the snowflake falling in the river.

Two squirrels chasing one another startled me. They nearly ran over my feet, then raced up the trunk of an oak tree in mad helixes.

"I know a lot of people think cremation is a good idea," Mr. Webster said simply, "but it's not for me." We talked no more about the tinny memorial plate on the tree.

Mr. Webster needed to get to Good Friday church services early that afternoon, and so we moved along quickly to our cars, finding things in common as we chatted. I mentioned that my father had been in banking as well, and we compared notes on how that profession kept its members continually involved in community groups and projects. He asked me about people with my name, Rogers, whom he'd known in St. Paul, and I explained how that family is not related to me. He mentioned various places he had lived in the Twin Cities, and Ken, who is well versed in Minnesota and local history and geography, made connections with several of the addresses. Mr. Webster's grandfather King had been chief of police in St. Paul; Ken believed he had just come across a biographical sketch of him, and promised to look for it and send it on.

We reached the cars. "If you want local history," he said again, "you'd be better off talking to my brother. He lives in a house in town called Graystone; it's a concrete house, built in 1905. You'll see it when you drive through. My father used to come down on a boat and spend his summers here. That was almost a hundred years ago." I wrote down his brother's phone number.

Mr. Webster thanked us for our interest, and I thanked him for coming out on short notice; and I hope that he knew, too, that I was thanking him for having been a good steward of this place. He drove away.

The sun was high now, and warm on our faces. Ken and I stood there gratefully. From the top branches of a spruce, a cardinal thrust its whistle into the spring breeze. The intermittent stopping and starting of a chainsaw whined from a distance.

WITH MY MOTHER
IN ST. BRENDAN'S CEMETERY,
GREEN ISLE, MINNESOTA

Two years ago
the steeple toppled but now,
like a windfall apple
put back on the tree,
it's been restored.

Partly to see it,
I've brought her home
to this church named
for the Kerryman who sailed west
into the ice.

It's cool for May.
She wraps a black sweater
around her, against the
chilling gusts. The sky is sunless,
gray as wet chalk.

We've brought begonias
for her parents' graves,
We place them with care,
offer short prayers,
cross ourselves,

and then head back,
stepping over tea-brown puddles,
down well-platted lanes
of granite. She reads them
like a childhood map;

today, these names,
none of whom I knew in the flesh,
prompt her to release
old secrets. She easily taps
a long-locked vein:

"This man: married
and had a family when he got
a poor farm girl pregnant,
out in the country.
She gave the baby up . . .

"Oh, Mother told me about
this one: he lived here for years,
and never mentioned a wife
until she and four children
arrived on the train . . .

"And over here—Maurice.
You know him; Eileen's husband.
They had get married, of course.
It worked out in the end, or so
you have to hope."

Then a rush of wind
threatens a word-drowning rain,
and my mother withdraws
from her uncharted stories,
bottles them up

ACKNOWLEDGMENTS

PHOTOGRAPHS: With two exceptions, all of the photographs were taken by the late David Tigan of Mendota Heights, Minnesota, who died too soon in January 2011. The photographs do not illustrate the essays and poems; that is, the burial grounds depicted are not those discussed in the text. Rather, the images (of a variety of sites around the upper midwest) display David's gift for evoking both context and isolation in the same shot.

The two exceptions are on pages 16 and 19, which show the headstone of James Charlis in Holy Cross Cemetery in Halifax, Nova Scotia, described in the accompanying poem. Those photographs were taken by Denny Haley of Wayzata, Minnesota.

COVER: The cover art is a detail from *Norwegian Series, Number 3* by the landscape painter Paul Damon of St. Paul, Minnesota. More of Paul Damon's work can be viewed at http://www.pauldamonlandscapes.com/.

I extend sincere thanks and credit to the editors of the following publications, in which a number of the works collected here first appeared. Our world is enriched by the dedication and persistence of literary publishers.

"Elegy" was originally published in *New Letters,* 67:4, Winter, 2001.

"Roads, Stories, Indians, Air" was originally published in *ISLE: Interdisciplinary Studies in Literature and Environment,* 12:1, Summer, 2005.

"The Old Order" was originally published in *South Dakota Review,* 41:4, Winter, 2003.

"In the Driftless Area" was originally published in *Big Muddy: A Journal of the Mississippi River Valley,* 4:1, Spring, 2004.

"At a Country Graveyard in Washington County," "Revisiting Oak Hill," "Near Plainview," "Old St. Vincent's, Houston," and "Translation" were originally published in the chapbook *Sundogs,* published by Parallel Press, 2006.

"To the sculptor who carved the headstone of James Charlis, born in Kells, County Meath, in 1796" was originally published in *Spiritus,* 6:1, Spring, 2006.

for fear of that rain,
falling in silent sheets,
rain that could have blown here
from Ireland. We've just felt
the first drop.